THE
Sacred
UNDOING

Copyright © 2025 by Martijn van Tilborgh

Published by Unorthodox Resources

All rights reserved. No portion of this book may be reproduced, stored in a retrieval system, or transmitted in any form or by any means—electronic, mechanical, photocopy, recording, scanning, or other—except for brief quotations in critical reviews or articles, without prior written permission of the author.

Unless otherwise specified, all Scripture quotations are taken from the New King James Version®. Copyright © 1982 by Thomas Nelson. Used by permission. All rights reserved. | Scripture quotations marked BSB are from The Holy Bible, Berean Study Bible, BSB, Copyright ©2016, 2020 by Bible Hub Used by Permission. All Rights Reserved Worldwide. | Scripture quotations marked ESV are from The ESV® Bible (The Holy Bible, English Standard Version®), copyright © 2001 by Crossway, a publishing ministry of Good News Publishers. Used by permission. All rights reserved. | Scripture quotations marked KJV are taken from the King James Version of the Bible. Public domain. | Scripture quotations marked NASB are taken from the (NASB®) New American Standard Bible®, Copyright © 1960, 1971, 1977, 1995, 2020 by The Lockman Foundation. Used by permission. All rights reserved. www.lockman.org | Scripture quotations marked NIV are taken from the Holy Bible, New International Version®, NIV®. Copyright © 1973, 1978, 1984, 2011 by Biblica, Inc.™ Used by permission of Zondervan. All rights reserved worldwide. www.zondervan.com. The "NIV" and "New International Version" are trademarks registered in the United States Patent and Trademark Office by Biblica, Inc.™ | Scripture quotations marked NTFE are taken from the New Testament for Everyone. Scripture quotations taken from The New Testament for Everyone are copyright © Nicholas Thomas Wright 2011, 2018, 2019.

For foreign and subsidiary rights, contact the author.

Cover design by: Joe DeLeon

ISBN: 978-1-964794-99-0   1 2 3 4 5 6 7 8 9 10

Printed in the United States of America

THE *Sacred* UNDOING

How Letting Go of Religion Can Lead You Closer to God

Martijn van Tilborgh | Jason Clark | Dr. Matthew Hester
Steve Chalke | David de Vos | Allison van Tilborgh-Martinous
W. Paul Young | Channock Banet | Tullian Tchividjian | Joyce de Vos
Dr. C. Baxter Kruger | Dr. Cory Rice | Keith Giles | Jamie Englehart

Contents

YOUR INVITATION: BY MARTIJN VAN TILBORGH 13

CHAPTER 1. SHATTERING THE ILLUSION OF SEPARATION: BY JASON CLARK 23

CHAPTER 2. WHAT ABOUT THE VIOLENT GOD?: BY DR. MATTHEW HESTER 41

CHAPTER 3. THE ONES WE'VE PUSHED OUT: BY STEVE CHALKE, MBE, FRSA 61

CHAPTER 4. HONEST TO GOD: BY DAVID DE VOS 75

CHAPTER 5. REDISCOVERING THE UNLIKELY JOY OF THE NATIVITY: BY ALLISON VAN TILBORGH-MARTINOUS, MTS 87

CHAPTER 6. FUTURE TRIPPING: BY W. PAUL YOUNG 107

CHAPTER 7. UNCHURCHING THE CHURCH: BY CHANNOCK BANET......................... 119

CHAPTER 8. CARNAGE AND GRACE: BY TULLIAN TCHIVIDJIAN...................... 131

CHAPTER 9. LOVE WITHOUT LEASHES: BY JOYCE DE VOS................................ 143

CHAPTER 10. LOVE'S FINAL "NO" AND FOREVER "YES": BY DR. C. BAXTER KRUGER.................... 155

CHAPTER 11. PERFECTLY UPSIDE DOWN:
BY DR. CORY RICE 177

CHAPTER 12. THE CASE FOR UNIVERSAL RESTORATION:
BY KEITH GILES 193

CHAPTER 13. QUESTIONS, QUESTIONS, QUESTIONS:
BY JAMIE ENGLEHART 211

PERMISSION TO WANDER:
BY MARTIJN VAN TILBORGH 219

Your Invitation

Getting to Know the Ambiguous God

By Martijn van Tilborgh

After forty years of wandering through the wilderness, Moses encountered God at the burning bush. The last thing on his mind was to return to Egypt, a land associated with deep trauma that he finally managed to lock away. He had thrown away the key a long time ago!

Yet this supernatural encounter would cause him to face his demons and deliver his people from bondage. However, Moses was confused by the whole situation. He had two major questions that needed to be answered before he could embark on his mission:

1) "Who am I?" (Exodus 3:11)
2) "Who are You?" (Exodus 3:13)

Moses was insecure about himself and his ability to get the job done. For starters, he wasn't a great communicator. He hadn't spoken much for the last four decades as he wandered through the wilderness herding sheep. Also, he wasn't too excited about delivering "the word of the Lord" to the man who practically raised him, especially since his message wasn't particularly encouraging.

Though insecure, God assured him he was the right man for the job. He provided Moses with a practical solution for his speech impediment by assigning Aaron, his brother, as his "mouthpiece" and gave him several "tricks" to demonstrate his spiritual authority.

The second question was more challenging to answer. *Who are You? What's Your name?*

On the one hand, Moses couldn't deny that the spiritual experience at that bush was real and transformational. Yet, at the same time, he was unsure about the identity of this god that was sending him on what appeared to be a suicide mission.

He wasn't confident in his ability to accurately articulate who was sending him.

It makes sense when you think about it!

Moses had grown up in environments that would have caused most of us to become spiritually schizophrenic, at best.

For starters, he was raised by three different sets of parents and cultures who each worshiped different gods.

First, there were his natural parents. However, he moved homes before he was old enough to understand who the God of Abraham, Isaac, and Jacob was.

In Pharaoh's house, many gods were worshiped. The most prominent one among them was Ra, the sun god. As a young man, Moses was indoctrinated with the idea that you really wanted to stay on Ra's good side, or else. So, picking a fight with that guy to get his people out wasn't a small ask.

Through a series of unfortunate events, Moses ended up in the desert, where he met Jethro, the priest of Midian, who adopted him into his family. One could argue that Moses ended up "unequally yoked" by marrying the daughter of this strange religious character. I'm not exactly sure what a priest of Midian believes, but it doesn't sound very "Christian."

From the context of his upbringing, the question, "Who do I say sent me?" seemed a fair one to ask. Moses got to know quite a few gods over the years, which made him wonder which one he was talking to.

Now, here's what I'm getting at: The answer God gave Moses regarding His identity was astounding and profound.

God told him in verse 14, "Tell them that I AM WHO I AM has sent you!" (Some translations say, "I'll be who I'll be.")

Wow, it's hard to come up with a more ambiguous answer than that, right?

Really? I am who I am? That's the best You've got? C'mon! You gotta give me more than that!

When you read the complete account of Moses' calling, you'll discover that God didn't fill in the blanks related to defining His identity. The answer remained ambiguous and impractical at best.

He told Moses not to worry too much about the specifics regarding His identity. He would just "be who He would be" as Moses would embark on his assignment.

The only tangible answer God gave Moses was that He assured him He was the same God of his father—the God of Abraham, Isaac, and Jacob (see Exodus 3:6).

> ## *Although God doesn't change, our perception of who He is constantly changes.*

Well, at least he got that out of his burning bush experience. Rest assured, the God his ancestors had worshiped was the same God he had just conversed with.

But what did all this mean? "I am who I am"? It's kind of open-ended, isn't it?

In pondering these questions, here's what I learned:

1) **We're all on a journey.**

Although God doesn't change, our perception of who He is constantly changes. This is true for both us as individuals and humankind as a whole. Throughout history, God has continued to surprise humanity with what appears to be an ongoing process of progressive revelation about the truth and nature of His being.

Consider this remarkable Scripture from Exodus 6:3 (NKJV): "I appeared to Abraham, to Isaac, and to Jacob, as God Almighty, but by My name Lord I was not known to them."

Apparently, God could reveal one aspect of who He was while another part of His identity remained hidden from that generation. In this case, God was known as the all-powerful one, yet by the name "Lord," He wasn't known to them.

God Almighty defined precisely who God was to Abraham.

He was the creator of all things.

Everything belongs to Him.

However, there was more about God that was hidden from him. Years later, some of the "more" was about to be revealed to Moses.

By calling Himself Yahweh ("I am who I am"), God tried to explain to Moses that there was more to be discovered about Him, things hidden from previous generations. Instead of spelling out the "more," Moses was invited on a journey of discovery that, over time, would reveal new things about God that were previously hidden.

Scripture teaches us that God "declares the end from the beginning" (Isaiah 46:10, NKJV), implying that we find ourselves in the middle of that same journey Moses was invited into—a process that pushes us forward into discovering more of who God is.

2) **God will not be defined.**

Throughout history, many well-intended people have tried to define God. Even Scripture has been used repeatedly to attempt to decipher and define the anatomy of the Divine.

It makes me think of the following verses: "You search the Scriptures, for in them you think you have eternal life; and these are they which testify of Me. But you are not willing to come to Me that you may have life" (John 5:39-40, NKJV).

Instead of looking at Scripture as a means to define God, look at it as inspired text that points us in the right direction, like lamp posts light the way in which we should go—light and direction for a journey of discovery that generations past have started and that we now are privileged to continue.

Don't look at the Bible as the definitive Word of God, but rather a word of God—a word that speaks of the unfolding story of the divine dance that God is involved in with creation.

The Bible is too small. There is so much more.

Please don't take my word for it. The Bible teaches us that it only contains a sampling of who God is. The apostle John puts it this way in the last verse of his gospel: "And there are also many other things that Jesus did, which if they were written one by one, I suppose that even the world itself could not contain the books that would be written" (NKJV).

> *Who God is always falls outside our existing paradigms, thus creating that relationship of ambiguity.*

Our world is too small to even begin to define all God is and what He has done, let alone what He will continue to do!

Who God is always falls outside our existing paradigms, thus creating that relationship of ambiguity.

3) **God of the past. God of the present. God of the future.**

In Revelation 4:8 (NKJV), John speaks about "the God who was and is and is to come." This could imply that the nature of God changes throughout time, that the God of the past is different from the God of the future. This couldn't be further from the truth! It's not that God constantly changes His mind constantly; rather, we change our minds about who He is.

The God who was. We can read the stories of how God interacted with the "heroes of old," how He surprised humanity every time with a more extensive understanding of "who He was" through the lives of His people.

He showed Abraham, who was accustomed to a culture where "god" needed to be appeased through sacrifice, that he no longer needed to do this. This was a revolutionary revelation that changed the trajectory of humanity.

He showed Moses a "moral framework" through the Ten Commandments that would revolutionize the culture of the day and would set Israel apart from all the other nations. He showed through the life of Jesus that what was true for the Jewish people was now also true for the whole world!

The God who is. Who God was to the heroes of the Bible has become the foundation of who He is to us today. What surprised the early church in the book of Acts when the Holy Spirit came on the day of Pentecost has become the status quo of our belief system today.

The challenge is not to embrace the God who was or even the God who is. The real challenge is to seek the God who is to come! The reality is that the God who is will become the God who was tomorrow. We need to understand that the journey continues.

The God who is to come. Like Moses, God invites us on a journey through which we get to be surprised by new aspects of "the ambiguous God," who is who He is—a journey that will allow us to participate with Him in seeing His Kingdom come to earth as it already is established in heaven! A Kingdom that transforms all of creation through righteousness, peace, and joy!

Yes, God is everything we ever believed He was. Indeed, He is everything we believe He is. Yet, all that doesn't even begin to scratch the surface of who He is to become!

This book is an invitation to join that very journey—to step into the unknown with open hands and a curious heart. As you turn each page, you'll be invited to see God in ways you may have never considered before, to uncover dimensions of His nature that previous generations could not yet see. Like Moses at the burning bush, you may not receive all the answers right away—but you will find yourself drawn deeper into the mystery of the One who was, who is, and who is to come. My prayer is that as you read, you will not only learn about Him but encounter Him, and that this journey through the chapters ahead will transform the way you see the God who refuses to be confined.

CHAPTER 1

Shattering the Illusion of Separation

Where Love Set the Table

By Jason Clark

A GOD WHO DOESN'T OSCILLATE

That fan was the center of our universe, our delight and torment—our reward and punishment. For the brief seconds the air brushed across my clammy, tortured skin, I knew to my core that God was good, and I was loved. "Oh God," I sighed blissfully.

Then the damned thing moved on, and I began to doubt. "Oh God," I cried out again, this time with notes of desperation.

I was eight days into a thirteen-day whirlwind Philippines mission trip with a handful of saints. Now, five of us—the boys—were lying on the second floor of a two-story tin shack on the side of a volcano. Yeah, we were on an active burner—in case the natural heat wasn't enough.

And it was hot!

The Philippines is the hottest, most humid place I have ever been. New Orleans in July doesn't hold a candle to its suffocating heat. It was unworldly, unrelenting, and exhausting.

Oh God, there's a universe of meanings in those words.

"Oh God," I've said when the world was right and when it was wrong, but for the first thirty years of my life, I said it as if God were an oscillating fan.

Don't misunderstand. For my first thirty years, I knew God loved me like I knew the sun would rise, and I knew God was good. But sadly, that burning "knowing" within my heart was often contradicted by what I was taught about God on Sunday mornings, Wednesday nights, and any other time well-meaning substitutionary atonement preachers held court.

From most pulpits, during most of my life, God's goodness was presented like a fan that oscillated. God was always good, even when He wasn't.

You know, God was good but also sent bears to murder children (see 2 Kings 2:24), turned women into salt while raining hellfire down on entire cities (see Genesis 19:23-26), ordered angels to kill babies (see Exodus 12:23), and, of course, there's the book of Job, where God seems to have made a death deal with the devil.

For most of my life, God's goodness was dualistic—it was both a reward and a punishment. As a result, for those first thirty years or so, I wrestled with many a disorienting message from preachers who could biblically manipulate the goodness of God to present as an oscillating fan. And if I couldn't jive with their punishing separation interpretation, it was likely because I just didn't have enough faith.

In retrospect, the problem wasn't with the measure of my faith. The problem arose because of a very large flaw in my God lens.

It's called penal substitutionary atonement. And there isn't a Christian in the Western hemisphere who hasn't felt the horrific crushing weight of this abandonment theory.[1]

DEREK TURNER: BEYOND PUNISHMENT

"The cross is not about punishment or wrath but about love," Derek said.

Derek is a close friend and, for a couple of years, my co-host on the podcast. I love Derek. He is a pastor to his bones, loves well, and can unravel theological knots while staying rooted in compassion and kindness.

Derek has an unwavering commitment to Truth that sets people free. I count it a privilege to learn from and walk alongside him.

---

1   Jason Clark, excerpts from *Leaving and Finding Jesus* (Independently published, A Family Story, 2022).

Occasionally, we would have a conversation that didn't include a guest but instead allowed us to revelate around the love of God. One of my favorite discussions was early on as we tried to one-up each other with the beautiful discovery that the cross wasn't at all the transactional, sin-focused horror story we'd been raised on.

Yeah, we talked about penal substitutionary atonement. You know it.

This atonement theory suggests that sin separates humanity from God. In this view, humanity turns its back on God through rebellion, and God, in His holiness, turns His back on humanity because He cannot look upon sin. The cross, then, becomes a transaction in which Jesus takes the punishment for our sin, which satisfies God's wrath, enabling Him to forgive humanity *if* we repent. This view emphasizes separation, retribution, and conditional reconciliation. And it's what most of us are familiar with.

The restorative gospel many are awakening to? This Trinitarian good news of union? It tells a different story—the original. When humanity sins and turns its back on God, God does not turn away. Instead, He moves toward us, relentlessly pursuing reconciliation. In Jesus, God steps into humanity's brokenness, bearing the weight of sin and dismantling the lie of separation. It reveals that God never leaves, even in our darkest moments.

If you're a visual learner, I'd recommend watching Brad Jersak's "The Gospel in Chairs." He juxtaposes the punitive distance of penal substitution to the healing nearness of union.[2] It's a game changer. But back to my conversation with Derek.

This gospel reframes the good news as one of union, not separation. It invites us to live in the truth that we belong to a Father who is always for us, whose kindness and love transform and restore all things.

"The cross wasn't about God needing a transaction (to be close to us)," Derek said, leaning in. "It was about Jesus stepping into our story, into our brokenness, and showing us that we were never separate."

Then Derek shared the phrase I've already noted. A phrase he's repeated faithfully on every podcast we've done together. And when he isn't on the podcast, like the one with John Crowder, I do my best to quote him—"God became one of us to rescue all of us."[3]

That thought was expanded in my conversation with Crowder, during which the dismantling of penal substitution and the rediscovery of a gospel-centered on union vibrated in every cell of my being!

JOHN CROWDER: THE PROBLEM WITH PENAL SUBSTITUTION AND A GOSPEL RESTORED

John Crowder has become a friend. He is the quintessential Tambourine Man and has been playing some

---

[2] Brad Jersak, "Brad Jersak – The Gospel in Chairs – Session 1," Filmed June 29, 2017 at Forgotten Gospel Conference, 29:47, *YouTube*, https://www.youtube.com/watch?v=N7FKhHScgUQ&t=3s.

[3] Jason Clark and Derek Turner, hosts, *Rethinking God with Tacos*, podcast, adapted excerpts from "The Cross," January 6, 2021, https://www.youtube.com/watch?v=OmuvBv_sQSM.

beautifully disruptive rhythms for a long time. I am thankful for him and his bold pursuit of the good news. John is thought-provoking, funny, and irreverent in all the best ways. And he's masterful when addressing fear-based theology.

Every word from John invites us to a Christ-centered message of love, inclusion, and cosmic reconciliation, and very few on the planet can dismantle penal substitution better than John. But our conversation wasn't just a deconstruction; it was about rediscovering and rebuilding on Jesus, the Cornerstone.

Jesus didn't save us from an angry God. Jesus is God saving us.

"Thank God... Baxter Kruger nailed his colors to the mast on this... decades and decades ago." John wasted no time: "Jesus didn't save us from an angry God. Jesus is God saving us."

For years, penal substitutionary atonement has painted a picture of a divided Trinity: a wrathful Father appeased by the suffering of His Son. But as John pointed out, this atonement theory doesn't align with the God revealed in Jesus. "God's love didn't start at the cross—it was revealed there." John continued, "Jesus isn't saving us from God," he explained. "Jesus is God, saving us from sin, death, and the delusion of separation.... Jesus wasn't healing God's view of us; He was healing us."

The implications of this shift are profound, reframing the cross not as a courtroom drama but as a cosmic act of reconciliation.

> ## How can we trust a God who needs to punish His own Son before He can love us?

I chimed in with my critique of penal substitution, emphasizing the relational damage it can cause. "When the only way we can get people into a relationship with God is to scare them, it's no longer good news." I continued, "How can we trust a God who needs to punish His own Son before He can love us?"

But that's what we were raised with—a separation-focused, fear-based theology that has shaped the Western Church's message for generations.

This fear-based framework also distorts our understanding of judgment. "Does this mean God has no wrath?" John asked, anticipating the pushback. "Absolutely not. But there's a difference between the wrath of a father and the wrath of an executioner. Even God's wrath is a facet of His love. It's against the disease of sin that destroys His children, not against His children themselves." This redefinition of wrath—not as punitive but as purifying—invites us to see God's justice through the lens of love as restorative. But more on that later.

As the conversation unfolded, the early church's understanding of the atonement took center stage. "The first 500 years of Christianity were dominated by theologians who understood salvation as a cosmic victory," John explained. "Gregory of Nyssa, Origen, Athanasius—these guys weren't preaching a God who needed blood to appease His wrath. They were preaching a God who, through Christ, reconciled all of creation."

This recovery of the early Church's theology is a transformative shift in how we understand God's character. "If God is love," John said, "then He can't act outside of that love. As George MacDonald wrote, 'Love loves unto purity.' And so, the fire of God is not something to be feared but embraced. It's the very fire that heals."

The West was raised on penal substitution, or separation, and thus the cross was a transaction, an exchange to satisfy a wrathful God. But the cross wasn't about appeasing God's anger—it was about healing humanity.

"The biggest problem here in the Western Church is this separation thinking," John said. "It's the idea that there's distance between us and God, that Jesus has to bridge this gap because the Father can't even look at us. But that's a lie."

John didn't mince words as he critiqued the idea that Jesus died as a substitute to endure God's punishment for our sins. "This idea that the Father's turning on the

Son, that Jesus is the whipping boy for the Father's wrath . . . it's preached as the gospel, but it's not. It's a demonic fairytale," he said bluntly. And I can't tell you how much I love John's bluntness. It's the truth that sets us free.

John highlighted the worst thing about penal substitution—that it misrepresents the Trinity by creating an illusion of division. "What happened on the cross wasn't the Trinity imploding on itself," John explained. "Jesus wasn't paying off some dark side of God. He wasn't fixing God's view of humanity. He was healing humanity itself." "Come on," I said.

And he did. "Jesus was healing the human race. He was curing our human condition," he said, describing the cross as an act of reconciliation. "He stepped into the depths of our decay, sucked it into Himself, and pulled us out the other side as a new creation."

It's a perspective that challenges everything about how we view sin, judgment, and God's role in our redemption. "We've turned the cross into a courtroom drama where God is the judge, Jesus is the defense attorney, and we're on trial," John said. "But the truth is, the cross is a hospital, not a courtroom. It's where Jesus heals us, not where God condemns us."

This reframing exposes the transactional language that often infiltrates Western Christianity. "Religion builds an industry on the concept of separation," John observed. "It keeps people striving, desperate, and insecure, always trying to 'get closer to God.' But union means there is no distance to close. Jesus already brought us into the fullness of relationship with the Father."

John's thoughts reminded me of my friend and podcast guest, Carlos Padilla's statement, "Jesus didn't come to start a new religion. He came to end religion."[4] Man, that's good!

My heart burned; this is the gospel I have been growing sure of for years, and John has a way of describing it so we might be set free.

If Jesus is perfect theology, I thought, *then union is perfect theology.* Penal substitutionary atonement is built on separation, but the gospel is union. It's about a God who has always been with us, always been within us, always loved us, and always worked to heal us. And we are awakening to this reality—this finished work.

John's critique invites us to rediscover the beauty, depth, and power of the cross. It's not a transaction to appease a distant God. It's the ultimate act of love from a God who has stepped into our delusion of separation and revealed a Love that never leaves.

C. BAXTER KRUGER: A TRINITARIAN LOVE STORY

I know Baxter is getting serious billing early in this book, but for me, he is one of the foundational voices declaring this Greater Love, Trinitarian good news.

---

[4] Jason Clark and Derek Turner, hosts, *Rethinking God with Tacos*, podcast, adapted excerpts from "Carlos Padilla / Walking in God's Power," May 5, 2021, https://www.youtube.com/watch?v=WSnC9SiBiIs&list=PLgimV9UoSbAIbXX447Gu_5-kGpLAO_eJO&index=146.

So, grab your chair and hang on; this is about to get even better!

In my second podcast conversation with Baxter, we dove into the cross—not just as a historical moment but as a cosmic event that redefines everything we think we know about God and ourselves. "The cross is not a transaction to fix a legal problem," Baxter began, his voice steady yet passionate. It's a divine descent into our delusion, a rescue mission to meet us where we are."

He continued. "The Father, Son, and Spirit aren't spectators of human suffering; they're participants. Where was God when Christ was being crucified? God was in Christ. The Father wasn't distant, watching from the sidelines. The Father was in Jesus, holding Him and holding us."

Baxter's insistence that the cross reveals union rather than separation flips many of our Western Evangelical assumptions. "You actually believe Jesus had to pay the Father off?" an Orthodox bishop rhetorically asked him many years ago. "That has never crossed the mind of the early Church. The cross isn't about appeasing wrath; it's about stepping into our darkness and bringing us home."

This shift in understanding the cross transforms how we see God. "When we damn Him, crucify Him, hoist Him up on the cross, what does the Father say? He says, 'I am holding my Son and my wayward children in everlasting mercy.' That's who God is. The cross is the ultimate revelation of the Father's heart."

Imagining the question Baxter's statement would raise with podcast listeners, I asked, "What about the wrath of God—something that has shaped so much of modern theology?" Baxter paused thoughtfully before replying, "Wrath isn't God's anger at Jesus. Wrath is God's opposition to our destruction. It's His 'no' to our delusion and death and His 'yes' to our redemption. The cross is where that 'no' and 'yes' meet."

Baxter's vision of the cross includes a profound understanding of Christ's solidarity with humanity. "Jesus doesn't come to stand outside of us and point the way," he said. "He comes to become one with us, to step inside our brokenness and carry us out of it. He unites Himself with His bride in her delusion to deliver her."

The cross, in Baxter's words, is also deeply Trinitarian. "The Father, Son, and Spirit are indivisible," he explained. "When Jesus says, 'The Father is in me, and I am in the Father,' He's showing us that even on the cross, there is no separation. The whole Trinity is in this together, redeeming humanity from the inside out."

The cross isn't the end of the story; it's the beginning. "When we murdered Jesus, the Father transfigured that act into a new covenant—a union with us in our delusion. The light shines in the darkness, and the darkness doesn't understand it, but it can't overcome it either."

As our conversation ended, I asked Baxter how this vision of the cross shapes his life. He smiled and said, "You can't unsee it. Once you know the cross isn't about separation but union, you realize God has always been with us, even in our worst moments. The cross is God saying, 'I won't leave you. I am here. And I am making all things new.'"[56]

"I won't leave you." Those words burn with the gospel truth.

What if the cross is not a story where the Father looks away, but instead is a revelation that there is no shadow of turning in the Trinity?

NOR HAS HE HIDDEN HIS FACE

"A time is coming and in fact has come when you will be scattered, each to your own home. You will leave me all alone. Yet I am not alone, for my Father is with me" (John 16:32, NIV). Jesus spoke those words to His disciples before going to the cross.

That statement seems straightforward. The Father wasn't going anywhere—but if that's true, what do we do with Jesus's anguished cry on the cross: "My God, my God, why have You forsaken Me?" (Matthew 27:46, NKJV).

If I said, "Our Father [who] art in heaven," most of you would continue with the next verse, "Hallowed be thy name" (Matthew 6:9, KJV).

---

5 Jason Clark and Derek Turner, hosts, *Rethinking God with Tacos*, podcast, adapted excerpts from "C. Baxter Kruger / Jesus Meets Us Inside Our Delusion."
6 Jason Clark and Thomas Floyd, hosts, *Rethinking God with Tacos*, podcast, adapted excerpts from "C. Baxter Kruger / Christ In Us!"

If I sang, "Baby, I'm just gonna shake, shake, shake, shake, shake," my wife and kids would sing, "Shake it off, shake it off."[7]

When Jesus, battered and broken, nailed to a cross and feeling the desperation of our loneliness and the ache of abandonment, cried out, "My God, my God, why have You forsaken Me?" everyone who knows Scripture looked up Psalm 22:1.

That's because Jesus quoted the first verse of the poet king, David.

In Jesus's day, it was culturally understood that when a teacher quoted the first verse of a Psalm, he intended to draw the listener's attention to the Psalm in its entirety. And every Jewish person could quote the following verse of Psalm 22 by memory, and the one after that, and the one after that....

As Davidic Psalms go, Psalm 22 is pretty standard. David wrestled through life's mountaintops and valleys with the raw authenticity that makes him an Old Testament favorite—except on this day, Psalm 22 became powerfully prophetic. On this day, David's words came to horrific life before their very eyes.

"My God my God, why have You forsaken Me," is followed a few verses later by (NIV):

> *"All who see me mock me, they hurl insults...."* (v. 7)

---

7 Taylor Swift, vocalist, "Shake It Off," by Taylor Swift, Shellback, and Martin Max, August 18, 2014, track 6 on 1989, Big Machine.

"I am poured out like water, and all my bones are out of joint...." (v. 14)

"My mouth is dried up like a potsherd, and my tongue sticks to the roof of my mouth...." (v. 15)

"Dogs surround me, a pack of villains encircles me; they pierce my hands and my feet...." (v. 16)

"All my bones are on display; people stare and gloat over me...." (v. 17)

"They divide my clothes among them and cast lots for my garment...." (v. 18)

Then, in verse 24, the psalm prophetically reveals the nature of God and the relational dynamics taking place between Jesus and His Father on the cross. "He has not despised nor abhorred the affliction of the afflicted; **Nor has He hidden His face from Him**; But when He cried to Him for help, He heard" (Psalm 22:24, NKJV, emphasis added).

Jesus stepped inside Adam's delusion and experienced our sense of abandonment.

Jesus, on a cross, in His darkest hour, experiencing the devastating betrayal behind the lie that has oppressed all humanity—the lie that God abandons, forsakes, and leaves—quotes a scripture that reveals the power of the gospel unto salvation: GOD DOES NOT LEAVE. GOD HAS NEVER LEFT.

The Father did not leave, never has. As the old hymn writer wrote: "There is no shadow of turning with Thee." At that moment, God was in Christ, on a cross, reconciling all humanity to Himself! (see 2 Corinthians 5:19)

Jesus, fully God and fully man, cried out, "My God, my God, why have you forsaken Me?" And it was our cry—yours and mine—a cry to know a Love that would never leave or forsake us; a cry birthed from the delusion of separation that tracks all the way back to Adam. Jesus stepped inside Adam's delusion and experienced our sense of abandonment. And in that moment, He cried out in a desperation that every one of us has felt, *"My God, my God, why would you leave?"*

And at that moment, the Father was with His Son; He hadn't left, abandoned, turned His back, or scorned Him. He was there. He knew His Son couldn't sense it, couldn't feel His always-good love, but He was there, loving His boy, proud of His Son, sharing His agony, and enduring the cross for the joy on the other side. He was there forgiving, and reconciling, and not counting our cruel and punishing beliefs and delusions about Him against us.

Jesus's next words were powerful: *"It is finished"* (John 19:30, NIV).

And the curtain of the temple, the veil that represented humanity's cruel and punishing thoughts about a God who abandons—a God who separates Himself from us—was torn in two (see Matthew 27:51).

Jesus then called out in a loud voice, "'Father, into Your hands I commit My spirit.' When He had said this, He breathed His last" (Luke 23:46, NIV).

Jesus knew He wasn't alone, and He called God, 'Dad.'"[8]

A good Father does not leave, and Jesus knew this. His faith was firmly placed in the Truth that "neither death nor life, neither angels nor demons, neither the present nor the future, nor any powers, neither height nor depth, nor anything else in all creation, will be able to separate us from the love of God that is in Christ Jesus our Lord" (Romans 8:38-39, NIV).

By the way, that's where we place our faith—in the sure foundation of a Greater Love that never leaves.

Jesus revealed that regardless of our perspective, experience, ideology, or theology, our Father never leaves. Greater Love never abandons us. There is no separation in the nature of the Trinity, only in the mind and perception of humanity.[9]

> *Once you were alienated from God and were enemies in your minds because of your evil behavior. But now he has reconciled you by Christ's physical body through death*

---

8 Jason Clark, adapted from *Leaving and Finding Jesus*.
9 Jason Clark, adapted from *Prone to Love* (Shippensburg, PA: Destiny Image Publishers, 2014).

> to present you holy in his sight, without blemish and free from accusation. —Colossians 1:21-23 (NIV)

Dear friends, separation is not the gospel Jesus gave us. On the cross, a Triune God, in Christ, reconciled the world to Himself, *"not counting our sins against us"* (see 2 Corinthians 5:19).

On the cross, Jesus said, *"Father, forgive them; for they know not what they do"* (Luke 23:34, NKJV).

Then, before His last breath, He said, *"It is finished."*

Separation is not part of God's nature. There is no veil between heaven and earth—between God and humanity. That's why we call it the *good* news!

The cross is the ultimate act of love, redemption, and union.[10]

---

[10] Full chapter adapted from Jason Clark, *Rethinking God with Tacos: Reclaiming the Gospel of Love* (Unorthodox Resources, 2025).

CHAPTER 2

What About the Violent God?

Reconciling the God of War with the God of the Cross

By Dr. Matthew Hester

There's certainly no denying that the Bible, the Old Testament especially, is full of horrifically violent images. We have examples such as Cain murdering Abel, Noah's Flood, copious amounts of animal sacrifices, slavery, and the overwhelming cruelty and collateral damage of long-lasting campaigns of war. At surface level, we could agree that this is how humanity always prefers to advance itself, but it's particularly problematic in Scripture when we see God Himself commanding such acts. There then exists a dramatic tension that confronts every Christian believer and Interpreter of Scripture: on the one hand, we encounter Old Testament stories of God seeming to command horrendous acts of violence. On the other hand, we read the unequivocally nonviolent teachings of Jesus in the New Testament. Reconciling these two has challenged Christians and theologians for two millennia.

The Old Testament narrates Israel's journey of discovering their God, an evolving process that shapes their understanding. While God remains unchanged, Israel's perception of Him evolves, leading to certain assumptions, like attributing violent characteristics to God akin to pagan deities. Over time, prophets like Hosea challenge these assumptions, asserting that God desires mercy, not sacrifices—a notion Jesus echoed in His teachings.

Between the apparent divine sanction of genocide in the conquest of Canaan and the Sermon on the Mount, there's a significant shift. It's not a change in God but in humanity's revelation of His true nature. The Old Testament recounts Israel's journey to understanding God, but the journey doesn't end there—it leads to Jesus. Joshua and David offer glimpses, but it's Jesus of Nazareth who provides the full revelation of God. David was a product of his time, but Jesus, as the Son of David, embodies the exact nature of God.

Viewing the cross as a mirror allows you to see beyond the surface of violent depictions of God in the Old Testament. It unveils the true nature of God, fully revealed in Jesus Christ. If you struggle to reconcile the violent portrayals of God in the Old Testament with the message of the cross, it may indicate a lack of trust in the full revelation of God through Jesus. Previous glimpses of truth were obscured, suggesting an incomplete understanding of God's character prior to Jesus.

Violent depictions of God in the Old Testament serve as precursors to the crucified God. In essence, these violent portrayals can be seen as literary crucifixes, offering glimpses of the historical crucifixion when viewed through the lens of the cross.

OLD TESTAMENT "PROPHETIC" VIOLENCE

Let's take a look at Jeremiah's portrayal of God, where it seems like mercy and compassion are cast aside for the sake of destructive actions (see Jeremiah 13:14). But if we believe that the cross shows us who God really is, then we know that God would never abandon mercy and compassion to bring harm to families. So, we have to recognize that this grim image of God reflects Jeremiah's own flawed, culturally influenced understanding, rather than the true nature of God.

A significant portion of Jeremiah's ministry involved delivering what he perceived as divine judgment upon Israel. Throughout his prophetic messages, Jeremiah shared over one hundred disturbing images. While some of these images could potentially be interpreted as less grisly, many others appear to be quite explicit. Did God truly bring judgment upon children (see Jeremiah 2:30)? Did He intend to destroy everyone (see Jeremiah 6:21)? Did God provide poisoned water for the people to drink (see Jeremiah 8:14)? Did He want parents to resort to eating their own children out of desperation (see Jeremiah 19:7-9)? These questions highlight just a few examples of the violent and gruesome imagery associated with God in Jeremiah's prophecies. How can we reconcile such horrific imagery with the notion of a Christlike God? Can we find the God Who looks like Jesus shining through such darkness?

Jeremiah 7:21-23 says:

> *Thus says the LORD of hosts, the God of Israel: "Add your burnt offerings to your sacrifices, and eat the flesh. For in the day that I brought them out of the land of Egypt, I did not speak to your fathers or command them concerning burnt offerings and sacrifices. But this command I gave them: 'Obey my voice, and I will be your God, and you shall be my people. And walk in all the way that I command you, that it may be well with you.'*

In the middle of a book filled with gruesome depictions of violence attributed to God, there emerges a poignant reminder of what His heart truly desires for Israel. These unsettling images serve as a stark contrast, emphasizing that God's ultimate longing is for His people to know they are His beloved, they are cherished, and they are most fulfilled when intimately connected with Him. Sacrifice was never His desire, nor did He ever command it. Though the above reference may pertain to animal offerings, it's reasonable to infer that humans were never meant to be sacrificial pawns either.

Our trust in the God revealed on the cross flips these violent and disturbing portraits into a two-way mirror. When viewed in the light of the cross, we can see beyond these grim reflections of sin to witness the compassionate God embracing Jeremiah's flawed perception of Him. This is why God assumes this unpleasant appearance in Jeremiah's depiction in the Bible. Seen through the lens of the cross, violent portrayals of God, such as Jeremiah's, become both captivating and unsettling. These images are captivating because they reveal God bearing the weight of the sinful images we impose upon Him. Yet, they are also unsettling, as they challenge our projected beliefs about what God is capable of and willing to do to His beloved creation.

Another example we'll explore is that of the prophet Samuel and his complex connection with violence. Samuel faced the challenging task of anointing Saul, the first and one of the least successful kings in Israel's history. He also played a significant role in the reign of King David, one of Israel's most celebrated kings. Despite their differences, violence saturated both kings' reigns. I have no doubt that Saul and David viewed violence as a means of conquest, but how significant was the role of Samuel in the bloodshed we see attributed to God throughout these narratives?

Throughout Samuel's prophetic tenure, it's evident how challenging it was for him to bear the burdens of the Israelites, Saul, and even David. While it's natural to feel anger, it becomes concerning when anger escalates to violence. Yet, we often overlook these questionable actions. Perhaps we assume that as a prophet of God, Samuel's actions reflect God's will, even when they contradict Christlike behavior. This is one of the primary problems we have when we don't interpret such images through the work of the cross and the Person of Jesus.

> Then Samuel said, "Bring me Agag, the king of the Amalekites." And Agag came to him cheerfully. And Agag said, "Surely the bitterness of death is gone!" But Samuel said, "As your sword has made women childless, so shall your mother be childless among women." And Samuel cut Agag to pieces before the LORD at Gilgal.—1 Samuel 15:32-33 (NASB)

What are your thoughts when you read the above verse? How do you feel about the prophet of God cutting a man into pieces? Now, you may reason that his actions are justified, and you may be right. You may also conclude that this wasn't God who did it, but it could still be viewed as a righteous act of justice against Agag. We might also observe that while it doesn't appear God commanded the killing of Agag, He was apparently okay with it since He didn't restrain Samuel and bore witness to it. Did Samuel have a violent streak, or was it God who had been violent all along?

Alright, full disclosure, maybe I'm just throwing you a curveball here. Perhaps you could justify this kind of horror if I provided a bit more context. What if I told you that Judges 3:13 shows that the Amalekites, along with their Moabite and Ammonite allies, defeated Israel to oppress them? Judges 10:11-13 also confirms that the Amalekites were among the oppressors of Israel. Additionally, Judges 6:1-6 reveals that the Amalekites, along with their Midianite allies, destroyed Israelite farms "as far as Gaza," leading to a famine. Surely, knowing this history should at least offer some context for Samuel's anger and desire for vengeance.

Understanding the historical atrocities that the Amalekites inflicted upon Israel sheds light on what appears to be God's command for their destruction through righteous vengeance. In fact, Samuel prophesied these commands and attributed them to God!

1 Samuel 15:2-3:

> *Thus says the LORD of hosts, 'I have noted what Amalek did to Israel in opposing them on the way when they came up out of Egypt. Now go and strike Amalek and devote to destruction all that they have. Do not spare them, but kill both man and woman, child and infant, ox and sheep, camel and donkey.'"*

Here's a more comprehensive understanding of the situation: Amalek had a long history of persecuting Israel, and Samuel prophesied that it was time for them to face severe consequences. As you continue reading 1 Samuel 15, you discover that Saul failed to fully carry out God's command. Instead of completely destroying everything as instructed, he spared King Agag and allowed his people to keep some of the spoils of war to offer as sacrifices to God at Gilgal. Saul's disobedience, including sparing Agag and preserving spoils, ultimately leads to the gruesome fate of Agag and the permanent separation of Samuel from Saul.

All things considered, where do we see the character and nature of God that looks like Jesus in this story? I submit that we see Him everywhere. We see Him bearing the image of sin in 1 Samuel 15:2-3 when it's attributed to Him as commanding the destruction of men, women, children, and animals. This is the image of God being crucified. We also see God in 1 Samuel 15:32-33 when He continues to lovingly work with Samuel despite his murderous actions exacted on Agag in the presence of God. But where else can we see the character and nature of the Christlike God in this story? Between Samuel's decree, attributed to the desire of God, and Agag's being hacked into pieces at the hands of Samuel, we find a gentle and soft ray of light breaking through the oppressive cloud of judgment and killing, resembling the God revealed through the Person of Jesus.

1 Samuel 15:21-22 (NIV):

> The soldiers took sheep and cattle from the plunder, the best of what was devoted to God, in order to sacrifice them to the Lord your God at Gilgal. But Samuel replied: "Does the LORD delight in burnt offerings and sacrifices as much as in obeying the LORD? To obey is better than sacrifice, and to heed is better than the fat of rams."

In these two verses, placed between grotesque acts of violence, the voice of God shines through. He expresses no interest or delight in burnt offerings and sacrifices. His love extends to all that He has created, and His desire is for relational intimacy. The Father reminds us that "to obey is better" and "to heed is better." However, since Samuel and the Israelites show absolutely no interest in these gentle reminders, they immediately resort to using senseless violence to resolve conflicts. This does not reflect the heart of God, yet He continues to patiently work with them, meeting them where they are and addressing their beliefs about what they believe He desires.

Similarly, just as we witness God bearing the weight of the violent descriptions that Jeremiah prophesied, allowing Himself to be portrayed in various acts of unimaginable violence, we observe a similar dynamic in the accounts involving Samuel. If we remain faithful to a "Jesus Hermeneutic," we see God's people making Him responsible for the violence we crave. We also witness Him acting upon us when He bears these distorted images to move us forward in our understanding of His nature until we finally behold the pure image bearer who is Jesus. Simply stated, the violent and vengeful God looks like our "Rorschach Imagery," and the kind, loving, compassionate, and non-violent God is the true image revealed through Jesus.

VIOLENCE REPRODUCES VIOLENCE

We've caught a glimpse into the violent lifestyle and prophetic ministry of Samuel, but have you ever thought about how such violence can potentially impact others? Consider this: the two kings Samuel had direct ministerial influence over—Saul and David—were very violent men. Is this coincidence? It could be. But consider the words of Jesus in Matthew 26:52 when the Roman soldiers arrested Him: "Put your sword back into its place. For all who take the sword will perish by the sword" (NKJV). At this moment, we would protest that Jesus had every right to defend Himself, but Jesus demonstrates the clear character and nature of God to His disciples that violence never stops violence.

In light of this truth, it's at least fair to question how much the violent streak in Samuel affected those he was most influential over. The kingship of Saul was saturated with violence, and we may think that since Saul wasn't technically God's idea, Israel got what she deserved. But this train of thought is hard to maintain when we know that David, God's anointed and chosen king, was much more violent than Saul. Let's make sure that we're tracking together: Saul was violent but not chosen by

God; David was much more violent, but was chosen by God. What are we to do about this apparent paradox? What did Saul and David have in common? Samuel.

> *"Saul has slain his thousands, And David his ten thousands." Then Saul became very angry, for this lyric displeased him; and he said, "They have given David credit for ten thousands, but to me they have given credit for only thousands!"* —1 Samuel 18:7-8 (NASB)

I'm not claiming that Saul and David weren't responsible for their own actions—quite the opposite. I'm also not claiming that Samuel had some kind of nefarious spell over these men. But I do find it very interesting that people who have a propensity for violence tend to be attracted, empowered, and endeared to one another. Jesus, the perfect image of God, confronted Peter's violent streak time and time again. However, neither Saul, David, nor Samuel had enough clarity to break the cycle of their violent imagery.

VIOLENCE HAS A COST

Towards the end of King David's life, we witness a poignant exchange with his beloved son Solomon. In 1 Chronicles 22:7-9, David confides,

> *My son, I had it in my heart to build a house for the name of the LORD my God. But the word of the LORD came to me, saying, "You have shed much blood and have waged*

> *great wars. You shall not build a house to my name, because you have shed so much blood before me on the earth. Behold, a son shall be born to you who shall be a man of rest.... his name shall be Solomon, and I will give peace and quiet to Israel in his days."*

When I was growing up, I idolized David to some extent. What wasn't to admire? He was a man's man! A warrior, a womanizer, a king, but also a worshiper, and ultimately, regarded as a man after God's own heart (see Acts 13:22). He expanded Israel's territory like no other before him and was widely hailed as the greatest king in their history. Jesus quoted him. Jesus even referred to him as His father. Such praise! Such accolades! But, when all is said and done, is this what David truly desired to achieve or be remembered for?

David's aspiration was to construct a house for God, a cherished dream he longed to fulfill. However, God conveyed that due to David's history of violent conquests, he would not be the one to build it. This raises a perplexing question: Didn't God want David to vanquish Israel's foes? While there are instances where God may not have directly commanded David to engage in violence, His silence and apparent blessings may lead one to interpret David's actions as divinely endorsed. Would God command His beloved David to commit atrocities that would disqualify him from fulfilling the desire of his heart? Here, I believe, we catch a glimpse of the true character and nature of God. He is not a God of war but of peace.

We cannot help Jesus repair the world and build the true house of the Lord if we remain fascinated with the violent ways of David the warlord. It's David the worshiper that God makes his covenant with, not David the warlord. The warlord cannot build the house of the Lord. It's David's peaceable Son who builds the true temple.[11] —Brian Zahnd

DO YOU IDENTIFY MORE WITH THE LION OR THE LAMB?

When it comes to prophetic symbolism representing Jesus, two images stand far above the rest: the lion and the lamb. Which image do you most identify with? Which image most excites you? For me, it was easy—I loved the Lion of the tribe of Judah all the way. I adored everything about the imagery—the majestic mane, the large claws, the roar, the sharp teeth, all of it. I had an appreciation for the lamb too; after all, it was the lamb that took away the sin of the world. But now that the lamb has been crucified, resurrected, and ascended, are we not living in the age of the lion? Right?

Is Jesus alluded to as a lion? Certainly. When you examine Genesis 49:8-12, what do you envision for this descendant of Judah? He will receive praise from all. He will embody the strength of a lion, ruling over all peoples and crushing His enemies. Even His brothers will bow down to Him in reverence. His kingdom will be eternal,

---
[11] "Brian Zahnd, "God Doesn't Build His House by Violence," *Brian Zahnd (blog)*, December 6, 2012, https://brianzahnd.com/2012/12/god-doesnt-build-his-house-by-violence/.

unchallenged by any other, and all nations will eventually bring tribute and worship before Him. He is the one to whom all nations owe obedience. Pair these thoughts with the imagery John penned in Revelation 5:5: "Stop weeping; behold, the Lion that is from the tribe of Judah, the Root of David, has overcome" (NASB).

Is Jesus alluded to as a lamb? Certainly. John the Baptist publicly declared in John 1:29, "Behold, the Lamb of God, who takes away the sin of the world!" John echoes the same declaration a little later when he encounters Jesus publicly. The prophet Isaiah declared lamb imagery, reflecting the crucifixion, hundreds of years before the incarnation had occurred when he said in Isaiah 53:7, "He [Jesus] was oppressed, and he was afflicted, yet he opened not his mouth; like a lamb that is led to the slaughter, and like a sheep that before its shearers is silent, so he opened not his mouth."

There's no way around it; Jesus is both the Lion and the Lamb. But how do we identify with both of these images and the tension they represent? The first challenge we face is how not to impose our own expectations on either image. When we behold the lion imagery, we must resist defaulting to a great apex predator that tears its enemies to pieces. Similarly, when we contemplate the lamb imagery, we must resist defaulting to simply a weak and defenseless pet. Again, both images are true of Jesus, but it is His image and not our own projections of it that should define Him.

I believe one of the clearest ways to see the images at rest together is found in John's prophetic vision in Revelation 5:5-6:

> *And one of the elders said to me, "Weep no more; behold, the Lion of the tribe of Judah, the Root of David, has conquered, so that he can open the scroll and its seven seals." And between the throne and the four living creatures and among the elders I saw a Lamb standing, as though it had been slain.*

In this vision of Jesus Christ, we behold the lion and the lamb, but it's worth noting that John only heard the decree that the lion was present, yet he only saw a lamb, as though it had been slain. What do these images mean?

The Lion conquers as the crucified Lamb. This is who God has always been.

Jesus, being the Lion of the Tribe of Judah, represents His authority. It's true that His kingdom will be eternal, and all nations will bow their knee and declare that He is Lord. But how is this accomplished? Unbelievably, and contrary to our default methodology of violence, the Lion rules by being a slaughtered Lamb. The King of kings lays down His life and baptizes the world with other-centered, self-sacrificial agape to demonstrate the essence of His Kingship. The Lion conquers as the crucified Lamb. This is who God has always been.

MY KINGDOM IS NOT OF THIS WORLD

I want to make one more point in this chapter concerning the Godhead's non-violent way when it comes to our desire for power and empire-building. Jesus had a couple of very specific moments just before His crucifixion to speak to our perceived need for violence to defend ourselves or, at the very least, to defend Him: Peter cutting off the ear of Malchus and the conversation between Jesus and Pilate. The first example speaks to our personal need to take up arms to defend ourselves and others. The second example speaks to the temptation of marrying the gospel to the ways of empire.

> *The final miracle Jesus performed before His crucifixion was healing someone who hated Him and was wounded by the hands of someone who loved Him.*

The backdrop for Peter cutting off the ear of Malchus is pretty straightforward (see John 18). Judas had just betrayed Jesus, taking the first substantial step toward His crucifixion. Witnessing this completely unjust betrayal, Peter, one of the disciples who had heard the Sermon on the Mount and knew the ways of Jesus's love and forgiveness firsthand, drew his sword and did what most of us would've done as well—he started defending his Lord through violence. While blood was surely flowing from the head of Malchus, Jesus completely overturned this act of violence by the hand of His disciple. He healed and restored a man who wanted to see Him imprisoned at best and crucified at worst.

Consider this: the final miracle Jesus performed before His crucifixion was healing someone who hated Him and was wounded by the hands of someone who loved Him. This wasn't simply an isolated incident of Jesus resigning to His fate but rather demonstrating the core of His lived gospel, as well as offering another example of redeeming the distorted "Rorschach Imagery" projected onto His Father for thousands of years. God never needed anyone fighting for Him, nor did He desire anyone to perpetrate violence on another. He would rather heal and restore than destroy, always.

The backdrop for the conversation between Jesus and Pilate can be found in all four gospels. In John's account, we see Pilate speaking in the language of empire, which is the only language he knows. In John 18:33, Pilate asks the question that frames our perspective of two completely different systems of government: "Are you the king of the Jews?" (NIV) Asking this simple question is loaded with consequences. You see, Jerusalem had a king, and it wasn't Jesus; it was Herod. Any other king was a threat to his rule and therefore had to be exterminated.

When given the chance to respond, Jesus didn't answer Pilate with the language of empire, not because Jesus was in any way afraid of what others might do to Him, but because it gave Him the opportunity to proclaim truths about His nature and His kingdom that are completely opposed to the violent ways of empire-building that men employed. Jesus says in John 18:36, "My kingdom is not of this world. If my kingdom were of this world, my servants would have been fighting, that I might not be delivered over to the Jews. But my kingdom is not from the world." To calm Pilate's heart, Jesus tells him that His kingdom doesn't overcome with violence. This type of kingdom imagery was completely foolish to someone like Pilate. Let's be honest, it's completely foolish to our modern sensibilities as well.

Today, I frequently mourn how much violence is celebrated in our culture. And before you think I'm talking about the world, which should be a given, I'm actually talking about the prevailing violence you can find within the professing church! We are quick to fight, both literally and conversationally; we praise wars when we deem them as justified, and we crave the marriage of the gospel with the American Empire. This all goes against the spoken and lived gospel of Jesus. Thankfully, more people are beginning to see the image of God free from their own projections. Thankfully, there is hope for a generation that learns to war no more (see Isaiah 2:4). Thankfully, there is a fresh desire to put the god of war to rest once and for all.[12]

---

12 Full chapter adapted from Matthew Hester, *The Rorschach God: You Thought I Was Exactly Like You*... (Sanford, FL: Four Rivers Media, 2024).

CHAPTER 3

The Ones We've Pushed Out

How Bad Theology Has Turned Good News into Gatekeeping

By Steve Chalke, MBE, FRSA

We don't often think of theology as dangerous. It can feel like the domain of scholars and seminarians—abstract, intellectual, removed from the pressing realities of injustice, identity, and pain. But this is a dangerous illusion. Theology is not just about what we think of God; it determines how we live with one another. It shapes our beliefs about who belongs, who matters, who deserves help, and who can be discarded. When theology is twisted—when it reflects fear, exclusion, or the need to control—it distorts our view of humanity itself. It teaches some to see themselves as inherently unworthy, others as superior, and still others as condemned. And when that distorted theology is dressed up in divine authority, the harm it causes is profound: children grow up believing they are abominations, abuse victims are told to forgive and submit, Black and brown bodies are systemically devalued, and entire communities are driven out of churches that should have been their refuge.

Theology is never neutral. It seeps into pulpits and policies, catechisms and courtrooms. It influences how pastors counsel, how parents discipline, how schools exclude, and how governments rule. And when that theology is rooted in hierarchy rather than humility, in certainty rather than compassion, in fear rather than love—it wounds. Deeply. Not in the abstract, but in the lived reality of people who are silenced, shamed, and pushed to the margins in the name of God. Real people carry real scars from bad theology—emotional, psychological, and sometimes even physical. The Church cannot afford to pretend that theological ideas are harmless. They have shaped empires, fueled colonization, justified slavery, subjugated women, and driven countless individuals to despair. If our theology doesn't bring life, it brings death. And it's time we reckoned with the cost.

WHEN DOCTRINE BECOMES DANGEROUS

Consider Martin Luther—a theological reformer who reshaped Christianity by re-centering the gospel on grace. And yet, near the end of his life, he authored *On the Jews and Their Lies*,[13] a toxic, hate-filled manifesto. He called Jews "poisonous worms," advocated for the burning of synagogues, and laid theological groundwork later weaponized by the Nazis. Luther's legacy reminds us: even those who bring insight can cause immense harm when their theology is shaped by fear or control instead of love. When theology goes unchecked—when it's not held accountable to compassion—it can justify the unthinkable.

This isn't an isolated case. Scripture has long been misused to sanction violence and exclusion. One verse—"Do not allow a witch to live" (Exodus 22:18)—ignited witch hunts that led to the torture and execution of thousands, mostly women. The so-called "curse of Ham" justified slavery and white supremacy. Deuteronomy 23:2 was used to stigmatize children born outside of marriage. These aren't just ancient missteps; their echoes still shape theologies that divide, condemn, and exclude.

This is the cost of bad theology: fear, shame, and systemic harm disguised as faithfulness. When we interpret Scripture without context, compassion, or Christ at the center, we risk turning sacred words into weapons. Doctrine becomes more important than people. Certainty

---
13 Martin Luther, *On the Jews and Their Lies* (1543).

overrides humility. And the result isn't just confusion—it's deep, lasting damage.

We see it today in churches that once defended apartheid and segregation. But we also see it in subtler ways: in teachings that tell women to submit to abuse, that shame LGBTQ+ people into silence, that pressure survivors to suppress their pain. When theology teaches people to distrust their questions, deny their identity, or remain in harmful systems out of fear of rebellion, it doesn't lead to freedom—it leads to spiritual trauma.

Step into the shoes of an LGBTQ+ person raised in a conservative Christian home. Imagine the quiet unraveling that begins the moment they realize their identity doesn't align with what their church has labeled "biblical." The language of love they've heard from the pulpit begins to ring hollow when paired with selective verses weaponized against them. Leviticus 18:22 is quoted with certainty and severity, while other verses from the same chapter—prohibitions against eating shellfish, mixing fabrics, or shaving—are quietly brushed aside. What's being upheld is not biblical consistency, but cultural comfort cloaked in theological authority.

When lives are on the line, we're no longer debating ideas—we're confronting malpractice.

And the damage is staggering. This isn't just about doctrinal disagreement—it's about deep psychological and spiritual harm. LGBTQ+ youth from non-affirming religious environments are significantly more likely to experience depression, anxiety, and suicidal thoughts. For them, the church—meant to be a sanctuary—becomes a place of shame and trauma. Instead of meeting them with the love of Christ, many are met with rejection, silence, or conditional acceptance that leaves lasting scars.

Bad theology isn't just a matter of interpretation. It's the difference between feeling known or erased, between being welcomed or cast out, between choosing life or being pushed toward despair. And yet, churches often reduce these stakes to "differences of opinion," as if theological nuance outweighs human suffering. But when lives are on the line, we're no longer debating ideas—we're confronting malpractice.

The tragedy is that it's not only individuals who are wounded. Entire generations are walking away from the Church—not out of rebellion, but out of heartbreak. Many still love Jesus. They long for a community that reflects His grace and inclusion. But they cannot reconcile the message of divine love with the exclusion and judgment they see practiced in His name.

When churches teach that faithfulness means unflinching allegiance to inherited interpretations—rather than a living, breathing relationship with Christ—people don't just lose trust in the Church.

They begin to question whether God Himself can be trusted. Scripture becomes a tool of fear instead of a fountain of life. And the pulpit, instead of being a place where burdens are lifted, becomes the very place that adds to them.

MISUSING SCRIPTURE, LOSING PEOPLE

The crisis of credibility facing the modern Church is not, as some claim, the inevitable result of rising secularism or cultural decline. It's the result of the Church's own failure to reflect the love, grace, and humility of Jesus. People are walking away from faith because the image of God they've been handed is often violent, inconsistent, or cruel. When they open the Bible and find stories of God commanding genocide, or hear pastors defend slavery, patriarchy, and exclusion in His name, they don't encounter divine mystery—they encounter moral confusion. They're left asking: *If this is God, how could I ever trust Him?*

We've trained people to memorize verses but not to wrestle with meaning. We've taught children about Noah's Ark with coloring pages and cartoon animals—while skipping over the mass drowning of humanity that underpins the story. We've recited proof texts about sin and salvation without ever teaching how Scripture was shaped by culture, context, and human limitation. We've handed out absolute statements without the tools of discernment. And then we act surprised when people grow up, begin asking honest questions, and find our answers shallow or dismissive.

We can't fix this with louder music, edgier sermons, or artisanal coffee. People aren't leaving because church doesn't feel relevant. They're leaving because it doesn't feel real. They're leaving because we haven't been kind enough, honest enough, or loving enough. Because instead of meeting doubt with compassion, we've met it with defensiveness. Instead of sitting in the tension of mystery, we've rushed to protect certainty.

When churches cherry-pick Scripture—highlighting verses that align with their institutional values while ignoring those that challenge their power—they reduce a rich, complex, God-breathed library of texts into a string of doctrinal soundbites. The Bible becomes less a source of wisdom and more a tool for control. This doesn't deepen faith—it diminishes it. It teaches people to mistrust their instincts, suppress their questions, and fear the God they're supposed to love. And eventually, many decide that if loving God means abandoning their moral compass or their deepest sense of justice, they'd rather walk away.

To take the Bible seriously is not to wield it as a weapon, but to hold it with reverence and responsibility. It is to honor its depth, its contradictions, its humanity, and its divine intent. We must stop pretending that Scripture interpreted without love can still reveal the God who is love. Because when people lose trust in the character of God, they won't keep showing up just to sing songs about Him. They'll walk. And many already have.

HERETICS AND HOLY DISRUPTORS

Ironically, it's often those labeled "heretics" who help the Church find its soul again. Jesus Himself was accused of blasphemy and heresy by the religious elite of His day. Not because He denied God, but because He embodied God in ways that broke their categories—healing on the Sabbath, dining with outcasts, forgiving sins, and placing love above law. Peter, too, faced fierce opposition when he dared to baptize Gentiles, violating the purity codes that once defined belonging. Galileo was condemned for insisting that the Earth revolves around the sun—a claim that, while scientifically sound, threatened a theological structure too rigid to evolve. Beyers Naudé, a white South African pastor, was excommunicated and vilified by his denomination for speaking out against apartheid and exposing the theology that undergirded systemic racism.

These weren't enemies of the Church. They were its reformers. They loved the Church enough to confront it. They believed too deeply in the gospel to let it be twisted by fear, nationalism, or legalism. They saw where Christ was being eclipsed by control—and they spoke up. They put conscience over comfort, conviction over conformity, truth over tradition. Their path was often costly: loss of reputation, relationships, and roles. But their courage carved out space for the gospel to breathe again. They became the prophets we revere in hindsight—those who were right too soon.

The pattern continues. Reform rarely comes from the center of power. It is born on the margins—from women pushing against the stained-glass ceiling to pastors who dare to bless same-sex couples, to theologians reimagining God in ways that include rather than exclude. These voices are still too often dismissed as divisive or dangerous—not because they lack faith, but because their faith refuses to be confined by old fears. Yet history tells us the Church has always needed these brave disruptors. Not to destroy the Church, but to save it from shrinking into irrelevance, from hardening into dogma, from losing the heart of Christ.

When we confuse loyalty to tradition with loyalty to God, we resist the very Spirit we claim to follow. But courageous reformers show us a different way. They remind us that true faithfulness sometimes looks like dissent. That holiness sometimes looks like disruption. That the Spirit of God still moves—still challenges, still speaks, still reforms. And thank God for that. Because if the Church is to have a future, it will be because someone dared to ask, *Is this still what Jesus looks like?* and had the courage to change when the answer was no.

LOVE: THE ULTIMATE LITMUS TEST

So, how do we know whether a theology is good or bad? The Bible gives us a remarkably clear, radical standard: "God is love" (1 John 4:16). Not control. Not condemnation. Not tribalism or fear. Love. This isn't soft or sentimental—it's the central revelation of who God is. Love is not one of God's many attributes; it is the essence of His nature. And if our theology doesn't reflect that love, then no matter how orthodox or historical it may seem, it is missing the mark.

If our theology leads us to shame others, to marginalize them, to preserve hierarchies that keep people out—it is not of God. If it causes fear, erodes dignity, or places barriers between people and the grace of Christ, then it is bearing bad fruit. But if it leads to compassion, justice, reconciliation, and belonging—if it dignifies the image of God in the other—it reflects the heart of the gospel.

> *Jesus showed us that the highest form of holiness is not doctrinal precision, but radical, embodied love.*

Jesus modeled this hermeneutic with astonishing clarity. He healed on the Sabbath, not to defy the law but to fulfill it with love. He touched those the law called unclean. He dignified women in a culture that erased them. He forgave sinners before they repented. And when He quoted Leviticus, it wasn't to weaponize it—but to elevate its heart: "Love your neighbor as yourself." Jesus was never interested in rule-keeping for its own sake. He cared about whether those rules drew people closer to the Kingdom—or pushed them away.

We must ask ourselves: Does our reading of Scripture move us toward healing or toward harm? Does it make room for people to flourish, or does it force them to contort themselves to fit outdated molds? Jesus showed us that the highest form of holiness is not doctrinal precision, but radical, embodied love. The kind of love that flips tables when systems oppress and kneels in the dirt when someone is about to be stoned.

Reformation, then, is not betrayal—it is reverence. It is an act of holy humility. It is saying: we believe God is not finished speaking. We believe the Spirit is still leading. We believe truth is not a fossil to be preserved, but a living reality unfolding in love. But it begins with honesty. It begins with repentance—not in vague, safe terms, but with real confession. Real accountability. Real change.

We must examine every cherished belief and ask: *Is this still bearing good fruit? Does this still look like Jesus?* If not, it's time to let it go. This is not a call to dismiss Scripture. It's a call to take it seriously—so seriously that we refuse to use it as a weapon and insist on reading it through the lens of the One who is the Word made flesh.

A theology that harms others is not a theology worth preserving. And if reform means being misunderstood or criticized, so be it. The Church has never been transformed by those who chose comfort over courage. It was born through reformers who risked everything to recover the beating heart of the gospel: love.

A GOSPEL WORTH BELIEVING

The gospel is not about control. It's about liberation. It's not about certainty. It's about trust. It's not about defending tradition for its own sake. It's about embodying a love that disrupts, heals, and sets people free. At its core, the gospel invites us into a life that looks like Jesus—not a rigid system of belief, but a living, breathing way of compassion, courage, and welcome.

Jesus came not to protect power but to dismantle it. Not to uphold religious gatekeeping, but to tear down the fences that kept people out. He came not to shame the broken, but to stand with them, heal them, and call them beloved. He didn't silence questions—He welcomed them. He didn't demand blind conformity—He called people to think, to feel, to follow in love. If our theology doesn't look like Jesus—if it doesn't make room at the table, bind up the wounded, and elevate the voices long ignored—then it doesn't look like God.

Let us be heretics if we must so long as we are faithful to the God who is love.

To follow Christ is to embrace the long, courageous work of reform. To sit in discomfort. To unlearn what harms. To resist the temptation to preserve our comfort at the expense of someone else's dignity. It takes humility to admit that we may have been wrong. It takes maturity to allow faith to grow. And it takes bravery to begin again—not with bitterness, but with love as our guide.

The Church is at a crossroads. Many have walked away—not because they've lost faith in God, but because the image of God they were handed was too small, too angry, too conditional to be trusted. The cost of bad theology has never been higher. If we love the Church, we must be willing to change it. Let us be heretics if we must—so long as we are faithful to the God who is love. Let us be reformers, not because we despise what was, but because we believe something better is possible.

Theology can heal. But only if we allow it to breathe again—if we let it speak not only from pulpits but from the pain of the people, the questions of the doubters, and the cries of those who've been left out for too long. It will take courage to love louder than we've judged, and to reform faster than we've hurt. But this is the call.

And perhaps, most importantly, we must never stop asking: What kind of fruit is our theology producing? If it does not bring forth justice, mercy, humility, and love, then it is not the theology of Jesus. Reform, then, is not a betrayal of faith—it is its fulfillment. It is the path to life.

Let us walk it boldly, with compassion in our hearts and courage in our hands, until the Church begins to look less like fear—and more like Christ.

CHAPTER 4

Honest to God

Embracing the Courage to Be Authentic

By David de Vos

History is filled with stories of men and women used by God. Heroes I look up to. Sometimes they seem almost inhuman, as if they've reached superhero status. "Well done, good and faithful servant" are the most fulfilling words one could hope to hear at the end of the road.

Until I again hear about someone else falling. Every time, the news hits hard, as if the Bible isn't already full of such stories. Once cast aside, some never truly recover. Every leader who falls is a mirror for me. *Am I next? Am I not radical enough? Still susceptible to the lusts of this world? When will I be stoned?*

Deep down, I know I am no better than the leaders who seem to fall. Deeply insecure, with a big ego and a drive that I must admit is sometimes more about seeking recognition than being led by God's Spirit.

So, there it is. I said it: I am far from perfect.

IT IS UNSAFE TO BE HONEST

For leaders, it's often unsafe to come forward with their imperfections. The reactions of Christians are sometimes harsh, judgmental, and unforgiving. And yet we are the ones who should be known for God's love, the possibility of starting anew, and the gift of a second chance.

I vividly remember seeing an interview with former Hillsong NYC pastor Carl Lentz. His scandal was so public that no one thought he'd ever recover. Now, in my opinion, he shares his story in a raw and honest way. Some might see it as another attempt at attention, but I believe him.

In that interview, he said something that stuck with me: "Leaders who live a secret life will want to keep that life hidden—especially when they see how I was treated the moment everything came out." His words struck me. To avoid the same cancel culture, many stay in the shadows. Until one day, it's too late for them as well.

I've made a decision: I want to tell my honest story. Not another superhero tale, but the story of a baker who became an evangelist. Who then discovered that behind the scenes of this oh-so-beautiful world, there are just regular people. Beautiful, but also wounded people, with human needs and habits. People who, in God's name, sometimes do incomprehensible things—things I don't recognize in Jesus. The story of an evangelist who didn't have it all together for a while.

BEHIND THE IRON CURTAIN

I wanted to do it differently. Brother Andrew, founder of Open Doors, once gave me advice over coffee: "David! If you ever want to tell your story, don't be so foolish as to write it yourself. Let a good writer do it." If anyone had the right to say that, it was Brother Andrew. He had sold millions of copies of *God's Smuggler*.[14] He was a butcher, I a baker. "The butcher and the baker," he joked, "who would've thought God would want to use us?"

Andrew's story was about smuggling Bibles behind the Iron Curtain. That curtain is gone now. So, what was my story? I preached the ABCs of the gospel and had the absolute honor of meeting evangelist Reinhard Bonnke, preaching for him and even standing in similar venues before thousands of people. In the Netherlands, I became one of the most sought-after speakers. But there are thousands like me.

And yet . . . wait. There *is* still an "iron curtain." The curtain of the shadow side of my own heart and soul. The place I'd rather not visit. The place where I sometimes doubt God—or rather the way organized religion portrays Him.

---

14 Andrew, Brother, John L. Sherrill, and Elizabeth Sherrill. *God's Smuggler*. 35th anniversary ed. Grand Rapids, MI: Chosen Books, 2001.

That place is barren and dry, a place with a shadow of death. My depressive feelings were hidden there, and I didn't know why. It was there that my fantasies and most sinful desires lingered. No, not *that* journey....

THE INNER JOURNEY

Jesus invited me to take an inner journey to the parts of myself I didn't want to face. Parts I suppressed or drowned out with one of my radical sermons. It became a long, grueling seven-year journey. It was unpredictable, scary, and uncertain.

I learned about human needs—needs we all have. The only question is: how do you fulfill them? Divinely, neutrally, or destructively? Why did I do what I did? Why did I crave attention so much? I cried countless tears seeking healing. If the Bible says God collects your tears in a bottle, then He must have a whole warehouse full of bottles from me.

I discovered this journey was far from simple. It wasn't something like, "Come forward, we'll pray, and tomorrow everything will be different." The message I had preached for years—and so desperately wanted to believe—was something I had to confront. This inner journey couldn't be captured in a quick prayer.

During my recovery, I realized I needed much more than just a "spiritual" solution. If humans are holistic beings composed of spirit, soul, and body, then I had to work on all those elements. And man, was I afraid to do that. I had been taught that anything offering an alternative to the simple prayer—which I had been taught was *the* solution to everything—was, by definition, of the devil.

For many of you, this might not be new, but in many evangelical and charismatic circles, this is still believed and preached. I painfully discovered that some secular personal coaches and therapists seemed to live and teach the gospel better than I had ever seen it.

In the midst of one of my deepest depressive episodes, I flew to Tulsa. There, I met with a friend and mentor who was also an evangelist. The coffee was good, the breakfast even better, but the conversations were the best. I found that when you approach people vulnerably and honestly, they often respond with gentleness and understanding—so did my friend.

Just before we said goodbye, he caught my attention with this remark: "David, the Church has always experienced different waves of the Spirit. There was a wave of healing, a wave of faith, and a wave of the revelation of grace. But the next wave will be the therapeutic church." I'm not even sure if he was enthusiastic about this himself, but I found truth in his words.

THERAPY IN A NUTSHELL

My first experience with therapy felt uncomfortable. I climbed two flights of stairs to an office space that looked more like a cozy living room. "Would you like tea or water?" the therapist asked kindly. "No, thank you," I replied curtly. Once inside, I noticed the box of tissues was already in place. I sank into a couch surrounded by fluffy cushions, clearly well-worn by previous tears.

I immediately felt resistance. What am I doing here? Am I broken? Do I need help? Aren't I more than a conqueror? But I also knew I had to confront the voices I had been suppressing for years.

> *If you spoke to others the way you sometimes speak to yourself, you'd likely have no friends left.*

We all have a beautiful personality. Some call it your true self; I sometimes think of it as the reborn part of us. That divine voice whispering, "It's going to be OK. You are loved." But we also have other inner parts: the ambitious career chaser, the rescuer, the know-it-all. And then there's the inner critic, who can be unbelievably harsh on us. If you spoke to others the way you sometimes speak to yourself, you'd likely have no friends left.

Then there are the parts that live in the shadows: the inner wounded child, the adolescent frozen in time, and the parts that try to protect these vulnerable sides—often through fantasies of success, power, or even sexual desire. All I had been taught was this: *This is sin. Repent. Stop it.* But no one ever discussed *why* these parts existed. What do they want? Why do they keep showing up?

> *Therapy taught me to look at every side of myself with compassion—even the parts I once condemned or suppressed.*

I learned that they're all protectors—parts of your inner world that once helped you survive difficult times. But these protectors don't realize that your true, reborn self can now—with God's help—take over.

And then there is generational trauma—unexplained pains often dismissed as demonic influences. But the only path to complete healing is deep love and grace for every part of yourself. It requires understanding, listening, and cultivating new, empowering habits to meet the needs of these parts in a healthy, healing way.

Therapy taught me to look at every side of myself with compassion—even the parts I once condemned or suppressed. This isn't weakness; it's a step toward wholeness and freedom.

If I had a shadow, an iron curtain I didn't want to face, then I'm sure all those fallen preachers had one too. They tried to manage it in the dark until the mess became so large it exploded in their faces. The result? Scandals that led to their public cancellation, leaving them and their families in ruins.

THE JUNK DRAWER OF THE SOUL

It's like a junk drawer or a closet—the place where you quickly shove everything before guests arrive. Or that garage, which slowly fills with items that have no other place to go. But eventually, the drawer, closet or garage becomes so full that the clutter starts spilling out. The drawer won't close anymore. The garage door refuses to shut. At that moment, you have no choice but to clean it up, whether you want to or not.

Even my audience had to relate to this—there was no way they couldn't. Once your eyes are open, you can't unsee the mess. I began to feel less and less at home in the political world behind the scenes of the church.

So, I decided to go all in: to be raw, to be real, and to hold no secrets. I wanted to tell the most honest and raw story possible—not another heroic tale. To do that, I knew I needed someone to help me articulate this with full authenticity.

I remembered that coffee meeting with Brother Andrew: "Don't do this alone, David. Don't be foolish!" His words stuck with me. I decided to seek out a secular writer—someone who didn't believe, someone who could look at this from the outside in. That person turned out to be Marcel Langedijk. He had written several bestsellers about celebrities and even a book about his brother's euthanasia. That alone made him refreshingly different.

SHEDDING LIGHT ON MY SHADOW

By shining a light on my own shadow, my Christian colleagues were suddenly in the spotlight as well—and they didn't thank me for it. While Christians may not burn people at the stake anymore, they certainly do so online. My book created a bigger stir than I could have imagined. An article in a national newspaper labeled me the "evangelical whistleblower."

See? people thought, *that world is full of lies and hypocrisy.* My book hadn't even been released yet; it was only announced by a journalist who'd read an advance copy. The world went wild: my phone wouldn't stop ringing, and within no time, every major newspaper was writing about me. My videos went viral, and I was sitting at the table on the country's biggest talk show.

Because people recognized themselves in my story. I received hundreds of messages from former churchgoers, trans people, LGBTQ+ individuals, and others who had been sidelined because they were "different" or "living in sin." In my view, these were the people Jesus came for—or at least, that's how I read the Bible. Unintentionally, I became a voice for this group.

I was excited because that Easter weekend, we had planned our *Simply Jesus* conference. *Wow,* I thought, *all these hundreds of forgotten people will come back to the church.*

Then I got a call from the senior pastor of the megachurch we were partnering with for the conference. I'll spare you the details, but it was an unpleasant conversation. According to him, I had tarnished the bride of Christ. How could I speak about believers like that? He felt a responsibility for the church and went to the media, declaring I was unfit and that the leaders I referenced—those who might struggle with pornography or ego—certainly didn't exist in his world.

When I pleaded not to cancel the conference, arguing that these church-leavers were coming back, his cold response was: *Those people are just bitter and disappointed anyway.*

CANCELLED BY THE CHURCH

It happened right before my eyes: I was canceled, and now it had become national news. It even made it onto Wikipedia. Then again, Jesus was also thrown out of the synagogue. When He cleared the temple, there must have been voices saying, "He has a point, but does it have to be this way?"

My raw honesty wasn't appreciated by everyone. I've noticed it's often those who haven't yet faced their own iron curtain who cling tightly to their ideal Christian values, refusing to embrace their humanity. And that, I believe, is the essence of the gospel.

Never did I imagine my message would have such a ripple effect. But it speaks volumes about this time, this generation. They crave real stories. In a world where you must ask, "Is this man-made or AI-generated?" people hunger for authenticity and genuine examples.

We often pray for new things, but when they come, we close the doors.

When the church closed its doors to me, I decided to take my message to the theaters. *Rauw* (Raw) found a platform across the country. Thousands came to watch and listen—former church members, LGBTQ+ individuals, and even Muslims.

My journey has softened me. Some might see me as a pushover, no longer radical enough. There are people concerned about my path, but I know my heart is now navigating a freer course. "For God did not send his Son into the world to condemn the world, but to save the world through him" (John 3:17).

Have you made this journey yet? Are you open to hearing an unexpected voice from an unexpected place? We often pray for new things, but when they come, we close the doors.

The essence of following the Way has nothing to do with how great your faith is or how perfectly you've fabricated your image. It's about whether you've learned to love—even when you can't fully understand where someone else is coming from. With, by some counts, 46,000 denominations around the world, we face the challenge of becoming one. Thankfully, being united doesn't mean being in agreement. Can you love, even when you don't understand?

I believe that's the gospel![15]

---

[15] Full chapter adapted from David de Vos, "Honest to God: Embracing the Courage to Be Authentic," AVAIL Journal, no. 21 (Spring 2025).

CHAPTER 5

Rediscovering the Unlikely Joy of the Nativity

Finding Hope When the World Is Upside Down

By Allison van Tilborgh-Martinous, MTS

*G*rowing up, my dad hated Christmas.
If you asked him why, he couldn't quite tell you when things went wrong between him and the holiday, but it was vaguely tied to two core memories. First, the year the Christmas tree caught on fire in their living room—back when people still lit actual candles on live trees (a wildly terrible idea, in hindsight). And second—and far more enduring—a lifetime of being forced to sing slow, somber Christmas hymns in a small Dutch Reformed Church in small-town Holland.

When pressed, my dad—who was also a pastor for most of my childhood—would just shrug and say, "It's depressing."

And honestly? I've found a lot of pastors who quietly agree.

Christmas is beautiful, yes—but it can also feel like pressure wrapped in tinsel. It's cold. It's gray. It magnifies strained family relationships, seasonal depression, and financial anxiety. The expectations are sky-high, but you still have to get up there and deliver the joy of the Lord like your life (and year-end budget) depends on it.

More than one pastor I've worked with has jokingly referred to Christmas as "the second Super Bowl"—second only to Easter, of course. It's a giving moment, a growth moment, a guest moment. And somewhere between the candlelight service and the offering envelope, there's a subtle but very real pressure to *perform it well.*

On top of that, the story itself feels . . . tired. It's been told, painted, preached, performed, re-scored, and animated a thousand different ways. Down here in Florida, we blast instrumental versions of "The First Noel" while spraying fake snow made of bubbles in 80-degree heat, trying to convince ourselves it still stirs something.

Let's be honest: how many times can you say "A thrill of hope, the weary world rejoices" before it starts to feel more like an obligation than a revelation?

Maybe you're out there reading this thinking, "I get it. I know the story." I know the virgin birth. The magi. The shepherds. The star.

But... do you?

When was the last time you actually *sat* with the story—not as a sermon to preach or a script to stage, but as a real, raw, deeply human moment in history?

Let me remind you of the cast:

- » An unwed teenage girl, nine months pregnant, far from home.
- » Her fiancé, who's not the father, trying to figure out what faithfulness looks like.
- » Poor shepherds, who show up with nothing but their wonder.
- » Foreign millionaires who bring impractical gifts and a bit of holy confusion.
- » A few barn animals, just doing their part.
- » A land that offers what it can when no human would.
- » And a helpless infant, swaddled in obscurity, rumored to be the downfall of the empire.

It's all completely upside down. And that's the point.

Because nothing about this picture screams "God with us." And yet, it is precisely this messy, misfit, subversive scene that reveals the greatest truth of leadership and life: there is still hope when the world is upside down.

Especially for those called to lead in it.

MARY: LEADING WHEN EVERYTHING FALLS APART

Think back to when you were sixteen. What kept you up at night? High school drama, fashion choices, a crush not texting back. If you were born around the millennium like me, probably your Instagram grid.

Now picture Mary—probably that same age—navigating one of the most disorienting, wildly inconvenient, and poorly timed leadership assignments in human history.

Let's take stock:
» She's pregnant.
» Unmarried.
» Far from being in control of her own narrative.

Her reputation? Shot. Her credibility? Suspect.

There's no plan. No mentor. No playbook.

And somehow, she's carrying—literally and spiritually—a calling no one else understands.

And just when it seems like things can't get any more complicated, she's forced by imperial decree to travel more than 150 kilometers while nine months pregnant. On foot. Through hills. For a census. Because of her fiancé's distant ancestral connection to King David. That's the logistical reason. The actual reason? Imperial control.

Nothing about this situation is ideal. Everything about it is strange.

And yet—she moves.

This is leadership when nothing makes sense. When the timing is all wrong, the conditions are all wrong, the systems around you are indifferent or hostile, and the people around you have no idea what you're really going through.

It's easy to lead when the strategy is clear and the spreadsheets line up. It's something else entirely to lead when the path ahead is unknown, your body is exhausted, your name is being whispered in gossip circles, and your only certainty is the vague memory of a divine whisper you said yes to months ago.

Søren Kierkegaard once defined faith as "holding onto uncertainties with passionate conviction." That's Mary. Not blind obedience, but stubborn, embodied conviction in the face of absurdity. Not because she's fearless. But because something holy is happening—whether anyone else sees it or not.

She doesn't get to control the timing. She doesn't get to choose the conditions.

But she carries the calling anyway.

And despite the pain, the noise, the social pressure, and the total lack of predictability, she keeps moving. Not because the circumstances are affirming—but because the voice of God once was.

Thomas Aquinas wrote, "*Love takes up where knowledge leaves off.*"[16] Maybe that's what sustained her. Not clarity, but love. Love for what was promised. Love for

---

16 Thomas Aquinas, *Summa Theologica*, II-II, q. 27, a. 4, ad 1, trans. Fathers of the English Dominican Province (New York: Benziger Bros., 1947).

the people depending on her. Love for the God who whispered something into being that hadn't yet taken form.

Mary's leadership wasn't loud. It wasn't public. But it was steady.

She shows up to the stable—tired, probably bleeding, surrounded by strangers, still reeling from birth—and somehow, she's still leading.

And Scripture tells us, "*Mary treasured all these things and pondered them in her heart*" (Luke 2:19, NTFE).

Not after things got easier. Not once the story made sense.

Right in the middle of the mess.

JOSEPH: THE STRENGTH TO SUPPORT WHAT YOU DIDN'T START

By now, it's no shock to anyone that first-century Palestine was a deeply patriarchal society. Everything—status, lineage, legitimacy—ran through the man's name. That's why Mary, at the end of her pregnancy, was forced to travel such a long distance: because, legally and culturally, she already belonged to Joseph—and his lineage dictated her location more than her wellbeing did.

Even the gospel story itself nods to this. In Matthew, we're introduced to Joseph not by personality or profession, but by genealogy. And yet, for a man who enters the narrative through bloodline, Joseph's real legacy has nothing to do with biology.

We learn very little about him—just that he was pledged to marry Mary, and that when he learned she was pregnant, he resolved to quietly break off the engagement. Not because he was angry. Because he didn't want to disgrace her publicly. Quiet strength. Steady character.

Eventually, he comes around on the whole "Holy Spirit conception" situation. He stays. He marries her. He names the child. And he raises someone else's son.

That last part matters.

Because in leadership, there will be seasons when you are asked to carry a vision you didn't cast. To protect something you didn't conceive. To make room for someone else to shine—even when the spotlight used to land on you.

Joseph doesn't fight for center stage—even though he was probably raised to believe he should. In nearly every Byzantine Nativity mosaic, he's tucked into the corner. A shadowy figure on the sidelines. But it's not because he's passive. It's because he chooses not to insist on a spotlight he was culturally conditioned to expect. He knows his role, and he plays it with strength.

That's leadership. And it's rare.

The most vital leaders aren't the ones up front—but the ones who quietly anchor the story from behind the scenes.

Are Mary and Jesus his blood? No. But are they his family? Absolutely. Because he chooses them. Not out of obligation. Not for optics. But out of love. This is what some call "chosen family." I'd argue it's also "chosen leadership."

Because leadership isn't always about being appointed. Sometimes it's about stepping in when you weren't expected to.

It's about taking responsibility for something you didn't create, defending someone you don't "owe," investing in something that won't ever bear your name.

Joseph could have walked away. In fact, every cultural script available to him probably suggested he should.

But instead, he stays. He listens. He adapts.

He raises a child who isn't his and anchors a family that wasn't his to begin with.

Joseph shows us a version of masculinity—and ministry—that isn't about dominance, but presence. He protects. He provides. He believes. He stays.

And in a world that celebrates bold visionaries and platform builders, Joseph reminds us that sometimes the most vital leaders aren't the ones up front—but the ones who quietly anchor the story from behind the scenes.

The world around him might have expected bravado. Instead, he offers belief. The culture around him may have expected him to walk away. Instead, he leans in. His job isn't to be impressive. His job is to be faithful.

And for pastors and leaders, especially those in second-chair roles, that may be the most radically important role of all.

THE SHEPHERDS: THE POWER OF WONDER IN A CYNICAL WORLD

It was just another night shift. A crew of shepherds, probably half-asleep, chatting quietly to stay awake, scanning the horizon for predators. The same old rhythm: protect the flock, stay alert, try not to get eaten. Then, a sound. A flicker of light. Something strange in the air.

One of them thinks he sees a ghost. Before they can confirm or deny, the sky explodes with some kind of mystical army. Not exactly your average workplace hazard. "Trippy," to say the least. They're terrified. Confused. But maybe . . . a little exhilarated? Nothing interesting ever happened to poor shepherds like them.

And yet, they're the first ones to get the memo.

The message is bizarre:
» The Messiah is here (like, right now)
» He's a baby
» You'll find him wrapped up and lying in . . . an animal's food dish

You have to imagine at least one of the shepherds took a second look at his snack pouch and wondered if something was messing with his perception. This wasn't just unexpected—it was ridiculous. The kind of news that should have gone to palace officials or religious elites.

But instead, it comes to the guys who sleep in fields and smell like sheep.

And maybe that's the point.

The Kingdom breaks in, not through power or prestige, but through proximity and perception—through those who are close enough to the margins to still be paying attention.

The shepherds don't overanalyze. They don't dismiss it. They don't demand clarification or credentials. They simply wonder. And then they move.

> **Sometimes the most faithful thing a leader can do is pause, behold, *and let their heart be moved again.***

They cross the hills under cover of night, maybe giggling, maybe stunned into silence. Maybe their animals trail behind, a bit unruly, disrupting the neatness of the stable. Maybe the shepherds immediately understood what the rest of us still struggle with: that in this new world, the small things matter most. That wonder is not weakness. That humility is not the absence of leadership—it's the starting point of it.

They didn't come bearing influence or insight. They didn't have a strategic framework. But they brought something we too often forget to value: pure, unfiltered awe.

In an age where leadership is often synonymous with certainty, vision, and control, the shepherds remind us that some of the greatest movements of God begin with interruptions and wonder—not spreadsheets and strategy.

They didn't have much to give that night. But they offered their curiosity. Their joy. Their movement toward mystery. And in return, they witnessed glory.

Sometimes the most faithful thing a leader can do is *pause, behold*, and let their heart be moved again.

THE MAGI: THE HUMILITY TO WORSHIP WHERE YOU LEAST EXPECT IT

The magi could not have been more different from the shepherds. Wealthy. Educated. Likely older. Traveled. Religious, yes—but not in any way that aligned with the Jewish faith. These weren't insiders. They weren't locals. They didn't share the theology, the lineage, or even the language of the story they were stepping into.

And yet, they show up.

Picture it: three rich foreigners walking into a barn that smells like livestock and birth. They step over animal droppings, past a dazed teenage couple, and into a moment so wildly underwhelming, it must have stopped them in their tracks. This was not where they expected that brilliant star to lead them.

They brought expensive gifts—frankincense, myrrh, gold. None of it practical. None of it needed in the moment. (Imagine trying to trade perfume for a clean blanket or a place to sleep.) And still, they bow. Still, they kneel. They don't correct the scene. They don't question it. They worship.

Which makes you wonder: maybe this whole encounter did more for the magi than it did for the Holy Family.

> *If you lead long enough, God will eventually bring you to a place where everything you thought you knew gets redefined.*

Because this is what wise people do: they know when to release control, and when to let awe take over. These men, used to being treated with honor, fall to their knees in a stable. They don't send a messenger. They don't schedule a meeting. They get low. On the ground. In the dirt.

This is what real leaders eventually learn—that not everything is meant to be directed, shaped, or fixed. Some things are meant to be witnessed. And some moments are meant to break you open in all the best ways.

Their worship wasn't efficient. Their timing wasn't perfect. Their gifts weren't exactly practical. But what they offered was what the world is often starved for: unentitled, uncalculated reverence.

They didn't try to elevate the space to match their status. Instead, they let the poverty of the place elevate their perspective.

That's the kind of leadership that actually shifts things.

Because the truth is, if you lead long enough, God will eventually bring you to a place where everything you thought you knew gets redefined. Where your wealth, wisdom, and strategy won't buy you clarity—and all you'll be able to do is kneel in the mystery and call it holy.

That's not a detour. That's the arrival.

CREATION: THE LEADERSHIP OF SILENT, FAITHFUL WITNESS

Saint Francis of Assisi, the Italian patron saint of animals, was the first to ever set up a nativity scene for Christmas in 1223. Prior to this first display, Christmas was often celebrated by attending a Latin mass service, which most attendees wouldn't be able to interpret. In lieu of understanding Scripture, many people experienced their faith through art, albeit a very different kind of art than what Francis had in mind.

When thirteenth-century art depicted the Nativity, it was often presented much rosier than the barnyard reality presented in the Bible. Francis was on a mission to bring the story to life through guerrilla theater. He set up the scene in a nearby cave in Greccio, Italy, where he assigned townspeople roles to play, such as Mary, Joseph, and shepherds who he had watch real sheep. Critical to his display with the inclusion of live animals and real hay, which he borrowed from his close friend John Veilita. He was convinced that without a live donkey and ox, it would not be a true nativity display. Why the insistence?

Isaiah 1:3 (ESV) prophesies: *"The ox knows its owner, and the donkey its master's crib; but Israel does not know, my people do not understand."*

Following the birth of Jesus, this verse was interpreted to refer to the actual animals that may have been present at the time of his birth. They began to play an important part in understanding the birth of Jesus as a representation of the world being upside down—and that upside-downness being our salvation.

The manger itself is not incidental. It's Eucharistic. The animals offer what they have—their space, their food—and Christ lays Himself in the place they turn for sustenance. A preview of the day He would become food for the world.

Later in Isaiah, it is prophesied that there will be a day when, *"The wolf shall dwell with the lamb, and the leopard shall lie down with the young goat, and the calf and the lion and the fattened calf together; and a little child shall lead them"* (Isaiah 11:6, ESV).

That child had arrived. And before them, lying in their feeding trough, was the one who would inaugurate the restoration of all things—including the natural order. Gone would be the days when humans slay animals for food, and animals would kill one another for survival. An

Edenic vision for the renewal of the earth was afoot—a new world ahead of them; one that, in many ways, is still ahead of us. Even as humble animals, they possessed a *knowing* about the truth of Jesus that humans could not, because it did not "make sense" to them. Instead of intellectual or theological platitudes, they offer Jesus everything they have, however meager it may be.

Whereas the "logical" human response to the "baby king" may be "*that's no Messiah!*", it is the "lowly" animals who know their true "owner," while the rest of us are blinded from the truth of the Nativity event. The animals bore quiet witness, offering what little they had. They didn't need to speak. They didn't need to understand. They simply made room.

And so did the Earth.

Jesus was born in a stable not by design, but by displacement. Mary and Joseph had been uprooted by an imperial census, far from home and far from help. They were strangers in a strange land—vulnerable, displaced, and exhausted. And every human door had been closed.

But the Earth did not close hers.

Ancient liturgy captures it like this:

> *What shall we offer Thee, O Christ, who for our sakes hast appeared on earth as man? Every creature made by Thee offers Thee thanks. The angels offer Thee a hymn; the heavens a star; the Magi,*

gifts; the shepherds, their wonder; the earth, its cave; the wilderness, the manger.[17]

When no person made room, the Earth itself did. It offered its cave for shelter, its hay for warmth, its ground for the cradle of God. Even the sky participated, guiding the Magi not with words, but with a star brighter than any oil lamp.

The created world responds to Christ's coming with hospitality. With alignment. With presence.

There is something deeply instructive here for those in leadership. Not all participation is vocal. Not all leadership is platformed. Sometimes the most sacred work is making space—when no one else will.

The logic of the Nativity is not domination or control, but quiet cooperation. The Earth and her creatures play their role with a kind of knowing that predates theology. They don't strive to impress. They don't strategize their contribution.

They simply show up.

And sometimes, that's the most powerful kind of leadership we can offer.

JESUS: GOD'S ULTIMATE REVERSAL OF POWER AND LEADERSHIP

What a preposterous idea.

A virgin birth? An infant king? A peaceful Messiah?

---

[17] *Idiomelon for Vespers of the Nativity*, Tone 2, in *The Festal Menaion*, trans. Mother Mary and Archimandrite Kallistos Ware (South Canaan, PA: St. Tikhon's Seminary Press, 1990), 257.

The birth of Jesus is the birth of the greatest paradox the world has ever known.

God among us—but wrapped in flesh.

Heaven on Earth—but swaddled and silent.

Weak, strong. Last, first. Born again.

The meek will inherit the Earth.

This is the Good News we were waiting for? This child? For whom? For when?

His parents didn't even have the resources to birth Him in a proper room. He arrived on the margins of the margins—born not just poor, but rejected, out of place, and entirely dependent on the generosity of others. And this—*this*—was how God chose to enter the narrative?

No armies. No coronation. No position of power. Just a newborn in a borrowed stable, surrounded by animals, a teenager, and her bewildered fiancé.

And yet, somehow, this is the beginning of the Kingdom.

Sam Chand has said that *"the distance between expectation and reality is disappointment."*[18] And I imagine the Nativity was disappointing to more than a few. Not because of the reality itself, but because their expectations were rooted in force, not humility. In swordplay, not surrender.

They wanted the empire to be overthrown—loudly. What they got was a child who couldn't yet speak.

But leadership has always been defined more by what we assume it looks like than by what it truly is.

---

18 Sam Chand, *Leadership Pain: The Classroom for Growth* (Nashville, TN: Thomas Nelson, 2015).

So how does God lead?
By letting go.
By stepping down.
By arriving not in strength, but in need.

And that is perhaps the greatest reversal of all: that the Savior of the world came not to dominate, but to dwell. Not to command, but to connect. Not to display power, but to become powerless.

No money. No weapons. No territory to His name.
Just a child and his mama.
And a band of interspecies witnesses.
Just Him. And His wonder of all things.
And somehow . . . that was enough.
Hope came from that in the most upside-down way.

EVERY DAY IS THE NATIVITY: LEADING WITH RADICAL HOPE IN AN UPSIDE-DOWN WORLD

"The Virgin today gives birth to the Transcendent One, and the earth offers a cave to the Unapproachable One."[19]

It's easy to become desensitized to the Nativity story.

Magi this. Manger that. Shepherds here. Virgin birth there.

The details blur with each passing year, softened by repetition and wrapped in commercial nostalgia. The radical edge of the story—the sheer absurdity of it—starts to feel predictable. And many of us, especially in

---
[19] Orthodox Church in America, "Kontakion — Tone 3, 'Afterfeast of the Nativity of Our Lord and Savior Jesus Christ,'" OCA – Orthodox Church in America, accessed July 21, 2025.

ministry, find ourselves relieved when the holiday season ends so we can "get back to work."

But what if this *is* the work?

What if the Nativity isn't just something we remember—but something we *lead from*?

One of the most common mistakes we make is chronologizing the birth of Christ—treating it like a historical footnote, something to honor and admire at a distance. We remember what He *did* for us but forget what He is still doing *through* us.

The Orthodox liturgy offers another lens. On December 25, worshippers don't sing, *"The Virgin once gave birth...."* They proclaim, *"The Virgin today gives birth to the Transcendent One."*

Today.

Not yesterday.

Not long ago in Bethlehem.

Now.

The incarnation wasn't a one-time event. It's an ongoing disruption—a living, breathing invitation to participate in the Kingdom breaking in, not just when the world feels upside down, but through us, as we help turn it upside down in all the right ways.

And here's the challenge for leaders: What if every day is the Nativity?

What if every boardroom, every pulpit, every tough decision, every disappointing budget, every chaotic staff meeting—is a stable in disguise? What if the manger is still showing up in inconvenient, unimpressive places, asking if we'll notice? If we'll kneel? If we'll make room?

This is what the Nativity teaches us: that peace doesn't come through performance, polish, or positional power. It doesn't arrive with status or strategy. It breaks in through humility. Through weakness. Through wonder.

It comes to unwed teenagers, blue-collar dreamers, night-shift shepherds, wandering outsiders, barn animals, and dry earth.

And it keeps coming.

To leaders like us.

Today.[20]

---

[20] Full chapter adapted from Allison van Tilborgh, "The Manger Is the Model: Leading with Radical Hope in an Upside-Down World," AVAIL Journal, no. 23 (Fall 2025).

CHAPTER 6

Future Tripping

Staying Present in a Fear-filled World

By W. Paul Young

Alice and Bob (not their real names) are one of our younger couple-friends. They know most of our family—no small feat because we have seventeen living grandchildren.

I got a call from Bob: "Paul, would you please talk to Alice? We saw our doctor a few days ago, and after a bunch of tests to diagnose the most likely source of her symptoms, he told us she probably has one of four diseases, each potentially terminal. She's freaking out, and she isn't listening to anything I say. Would you call her?"

I agreed, and as soon as Bob and I hung up, I dialed her cell number. She answered, and we began with small talk, catching up about the details of our lives. It didn't take long before she asked, "Why are you calling me in the middle of the day, in the middle of the week?"

"Oh, Alice," I apologized, "I am so sorry. I probably should have started with that." I paused. "I am calling to help you plan your funeral."

Silence for a moment. Then she burst out laughing.

"So," I asked, "what kind of music would you like? Any special songs? Anyone you want to make sure is not invited?"

At this moment, you may be thinking, *What a cruel human being.* But am I?

"Paul, do you know what I've been doing the last forty-eight hours? Not sleeping. I have been on the internet finding everything I can about these four diseases, and the more information I have, the more afraid I am." (By the way, it turned out the issue was simple and easily handled.)

Alice was caught in what I call future-tripping. Future-tripping is when fear and imagination get together and immediately produce impending doom, gloom, trauma, tragedy, or difficulty. It can be something as complex as personal financial ruin or as simple as an approaching conversation. It can be as grandiose as nuclear war or worry over what others will think about the dessert I made for the party.

A few years ago, during the pandemic, I began researching information on why a pregnant woman must get vaccinated. The more I read, the more concerned

I became (concerned is a baptized word for fear). One of our daughters was pregnant, and it wasn't long before I had an impressive stack of documentation supporting my conclusion.

On one particularly beautiful, sunny summer day, she and her husband were swimming in the pool, and I strolled out to talk to them. And would you believe it? The conversation turned to how vitally important it was that a pregnant woman get the vaccine.

It must have been the Holy Spirit, I said to myself, not admitting that it was actually my manipulation.

I laid out my argument, and my daughter listened respectfully.

But she didn't buy the fear I was selling. Instead, her response was honest and straight. "Dad, I just don't sense that this is right for me, not now."

Did I listen to her? Not at all. After all, I am the dad and smarter than she. I became more concerned and more adamant about why I was right and she was wrong. Finally, very frustrated, I turned to our son-in-law and said strongly, "This is your baby, too. Why don't *you* do something about this?"

I hope you are cringing. It got worse. I turned to look at my daughter, and tears were streaming down her face. And how did I respond? I turned and walked back into the house, justifying myself. *At least I told them the truth, and if she ignores what I told her to do, and if she and the baby die, I will know I did the right thing. I had spoken the truth in love, hadn't I?*

The opposite. I was justifying my fears and trying to control my daughter. I didn't trust the Holy Spirit in her, so I tried to play the Holy Spirit at her. Thankfully, it only took half an hour before I heard the sweet and tender voice of the real Holy Spirit speak to me in the deeper places of my soul: "Paul, I love you, but you can be such an ass sometimes!"

With their clarity, those words broke me, and I did the next right thing. I went back out, knelt at the edge of the pool, and asked my daughter and son-in-law if they would forgive me. They immediately gave me the gift of their forgiveness, and my daughter added, "Dad, I hope you aren't under the impression that we think you're perfect."

Future-tripping. Creating a fear-based imagination of a future that does not exist and then trying to control everyone and everything so that what I am afraid of does not happen. Read that last sentence again. Do you see it? Future-tripping and control are diabolical siblings. If you are a control freak, I guarantee you are also a future-tripper and that your life is riddled with fear from bottom to top.

Imagination is not evil. It is part of the powerful grandeur of being human and how God is by nature. When love and imagination dance together, we run; we have creativity, wonder, adventure, risk-taking, exploration, childlikeness, and even joyful planning.

But in that moment, motivated by fear, I chose to eat from the tree of the knowledge of good and evil, trying to convince our daughter, whom I love, that I was right and she was wrong. It wasn't about relationship and love, and it was not about her flourishing. It was about me. I was attempting to control my life and hers, and I had done it under the guise of speaking the truth in love.

What was my fear? I imagined attending a funeral where there was a large box in which lay our beautiful daughter, and next to hers a smaller box holding the body of our precious grandchild. The more I entertained that imagination, the more complex and suffocating it became.

I imagined walking back into a house in which she no longer lived. I imagined what our relationship with her spouse would be like. I imagined the grandchildren we would never have. This is insanity. *None* of it was true. *None* of it was real. Imagining something that did not exist was terrifying me, and I attempted to overcome my fear by controlling my grown child and her husband.

The delusion of fear must have the reality of love to pretend to exist.

Instead, I might have eaten of the tree of life. How? I could have walked out to the pool, sat down, looked at the two of them, confessed my fears, and asked them to pray for me. Eating of the tree of life would have resulted in all of us flourishing. In hindsight, I *did* return later to the tree of life. It was when I asked for their forgiveness.

Who are the real enemies? Let's be clear. The enemy of love is fear. The enemy of trust is control. The word enemy is much, much, much too strong. We are not dealing with two existing realities, as if two gods were fighting it out on the battleground of the cosmos or in the human heart.

Love and trust and, similarly, goodness, kindness, joy, and much more, all have ontological existence. They exist whether there is a created cosmos or not because they are grounded in the God who *is*. The God who *is* Love by nature. Love includes trust, kindness, goodness, faithfulness, relationship, and so much more. Therefore, goodness exists without evil, kindness without meanness, life without death, trust without control, love without fear, community without aloneness, and so on.

But the delusion of fear must have the reality of love to pretend to exist. Fear describes what happens when one turns from love. Control is the illusion that is born when one turns from trust. Both are an absence, a rift of nothingness, the mystery of iniquity and alienation, that we humans then name and empower as real. The result has been and continues to be catastrophic.

Have you ever, in your imagination, been to your own funeral? I have. More than once. And it really ticked me off that no one else came. Have you ever imagined being so broke that you ended up alone, living in a cardboard box under the local bridge? Have you imagined what it is going to be like when you see _____ (that person), and what you are going to say, and how it is going to end terribly, or even well? (Future-tripping can be positive too, but still not real at all.)

Here are a few gateway drugs to future-tripping: buying a lottery ticket, hearing your boss wants to talk to you, watching the news, being told you will do something great for God, or that something showed up on the scan, or a grown child saying they never want to speak to you again and on and on and on.

Eternal life is not on a timeline. It is the ever-present *now*. Think about it. Where and when is God living in and with you? In some imagined future? No! Your participation in eternal life, the life of God, is only *now*. You experience joy only in the present tense. At fifty, I finally understood that joy had always been my constant companion, and it was me who was leaving, running off into some fear-based future-tripping unreality.

> ## *We don't get grace today for things that don't exist.*

As followers of the Sermon-on-the-Mount Jesus, we must stop segmenting our lives into sacred and secular compartments. There exists no such distinction, except for those who need it to justify their behavior when at a distance from a cross. In our moment-by-moment encounter with the indwelling God, we do the next right thing with all our strength, trusting a wisdom that is greater than our understanding and letting go of the outcomes.

It is unsettling to realize God cares for the eternal and not the temporal. Business is temporal. God cares infinitely more for the eternal person in front of you, and you and all the persons impacted by your company, than for its success or failure.

To *live*, we must dwell inside the grace of today. Grace of the day is simple. Jesus and I respond to what is right in front of us. I won't entertain, and get caught up in, imaginations about tomorrow and how things are going to work out—or not. It is a fundamental choice to trust. What makes this complicated is my need to control. We don't get grace today for things that don't exist. In this present moment is where everything that is real and true exists. You, God, love, joy, peace, hope, kindness and on and on.

What about planning?

James 4:13-15 (NIV) says:

> Now listen, you who say, "Today or tomorrow we will go to this or that city, spend a year there, carry on business and make money." Why, you do not even know what will happen tomorrow. What is your life? You are a mist that appears for a little while and then vanishes. Instead,

you ought to say, "If it is the Lord's will, we will live and do this or that."

As you are aware, planning in the moment may be creative and empowering, an expression of your love/trust union with God, or terrifying and disempowering, largely because of your attachment to the outcomes. James is saying, "Hold your plans loosely." Nothing like dying to mess up a plan or a calendar. The will of God is not a blueprint hidden in a vault somewhere. Rather, it is the moment-by-moment relational love that is growing inside your union with the indwelling God who loves you and respects your humanness, including all that you bring to the adventure.

The world is fueled by fear, and its response is control.

Fear will not let you stay present. It will push you out of everything that *is* and into a place that does not exist, where you are alone (a lie) and in which your only resources are your own (another lie).

Future tripping is a thief, taking away today's energy, resources, and relationships that empower you to respond to today's real people and circumstances, and wasting it on things that don't exist. This is exhausting and not living at all!

To stay present is to trust. To stay present is to live. To stay present is to love!

The world is fueled by fear, and its response is control. Love and trust are considered weak and ineffective when indeed they are the only way to live that changes anything. Fear adds to the misery. Love effects transformation.

How do we live *in* this world but not be *of* it? We stop future-tripping! Stop it!

Better said than done, believe me. It has taken me years to do the work of letting go of control and resting into trust. Often, the god that we have believed in is not worthy of our trust, so we must go through a re-boot, a detox, maybe a bit of atheism, so the god we have embraced can be trashed for the God revealed in Jesus.

The future is known only and fully in and by the being of God, eternal Love. Human beings are incredibly creative beings. If you say you are not a creative, I will simply ask you if you have ever been worried about anything. If you have, you are a creative. To worry, you become a screenwriter, a producer, and a director. You hire the actors and control their choices. And, of course, you are the star, all in a tragedy about something that does not exist.

"The more Christian attitude, which can be attained at any age, is to leave futurity in God's hands,"

C.S. Lewis writes in *The Weight of Glory and Other Addresses*. He continues:

> We may as well, for God will certainly retain it whether we leave it with Him or not. Never, within peace or war, commit your virtue or your happiness to the future. Happy work is best done by the person who takes his long-term plans somewhat lightly and works from moment to moment, as to the Lord. It is only our daily bread that we are encouraged to ask for. The present is the only time in which any response can be done, or grace received.[21]

Similarly, in his *Pensées*, Blaise Pascal writes:

> Let each of us examine his thoughts; he will find them wholly concerned with the past or the future. We almost never think of the present, and if we do think of it, it is only to see what light it throws on our plans for the future. The present is never our end. The past and the present are our means, the future alone our end. Thus we never actually live, but hope to live, and since we are always planning how to be happy, it is inevitable that we should never be so.[22]

Likewise, the Scriptures are replete with reminders that God is with us in the present and encourages us to join Him there—resisting the urge to worry about a tomorrow that does not yet exist. "Can any one of you by worrying add a single hour to your life?" Jesus asks

---
21 C. S. Lewis, *The Weight of Glory and Other Addresses* (New York: HarperOne, 2001).
22 Blaise Pascal, *Pensées*, trans. W. F. Trotter, fragment 172 (or fragment 78 in some numbering), in *The Thoughts of Blaise Pascal* (London: Dent, 1931), p. 50.

(Matthew 6:27, NIV). "Take no thought for tomorrow. Tomorrow will take care of itself," he says (Matthew 6:34, author paraphrase).

I was once having lunch with someone who was recounting to me her many life issues, fears, and burdens. When she was finished, I asked, "Is there anything that you can do or are being asked to do about any of this in this moment?"

She thought about it and said, "No."

I paused for a moment and said, "Well, then, please pass the salt."

In that moment, salt was more real than all her imagined future catastrophes. She recently emailed me and wrote, "Whenever I begin to future-trip, I say to myself, 'Pass the salt.'"

Live in life. Walk in the light. Stay present to love. Pass the salt.[23]

---

[23] Full chapter adapted from Paul Young, "Future Tripping: Staying Present in a Fear-Filled World," AVAIL Journal, no. 21 (Spring 2025).

CHAPTER 7

Unchurching the Church

Breaking Down the Arches Between Us

By Channock Banet

What if I told you church doesn't have to look like it always has? Maybe we've been so focused on what happens inside our buildings that we've missed the whole point. What if God is calling us to step outside, not just in a physical sense, but also mentally and spiritually, to see the world and His Kingdom in a completely new way?

This isn't just a story about me or about the church I lead. It's about what happens when we honestly wrestle with the question, "Now what?" The gospel of grace is about knowing who God is and understanding who we are in Him. The gospel of the Kingdom takes us further. It calls us to take responsibility. It answers the question of what we are supposed to do with what we now know about God and ourselves.

The Kingdom of God is not made up of servants. It is made up of sons and daughters who choose to serve. Ministry is not a position or a title. It is simply serving. Ephesians 4 says the fivefold ministry gifts exist to equip the saints for the work of ministry. Ministry is not about what happens on a stage. It is about showing up for the people in our neighborhoods and communities. It means seeing the needs right in front of us and responding to them.

Jesus is not the Savior from the world. He is the Savior of the world. The Kingdom of God is like yeast. It is meant to permeate everything. We are that yeast. We are the ones who have awakened to our true identity in Christ.

PEOPLE, NOT PROJECTS

This shift in mindset starts with how we see people. Do we see them as sons and daughters of God, or as projects to fix or problems to solve? For so long, I was taught that we become children of God only after we come to faith. But is that really true? If Paul could stand on Mars Hill in Acts 17 and tell pagans, "We are all God's offspring," then maybe we need to rethink how we view the people around us.

When Peter had his vision in Acts 10 of the unclean animals and heard God say, "Do not call anything impure that God has made clean," he did not understand it right away. Later, when he entered Cornelius's house, the meaning became clear. Peter said, "God has shown me that I should not call anyone impure or unclean." That word "anyone" was a revelation for Peter, and it should be for us too.

So how do we see people? What about those who do not look like you, believe like you, or behave like you? If we believe every person is a child of God, then our mission is not to separate ourselves from them. It is to love them, serve them, and point them to the truth of who they already are: a beloved son or daughter of the King.

THE ARCH THAT CHALLENGED MY SYSTEMS

One of the biggest revelations that changed my worldview came during a trip to Guatemala in the summer of 2018. We were supporting an orphanage and helping meet the basic needs of kids who had been abandoned. One afternoon, while staying in Antigua, we toured the city. It was a beautiful place filled with history. One of the most famous landmarks was a yellow arch in the heart of downtown.

Our guide told us the story behind the arch, and it floored me. It had been built centuries ago, not as decoration or architecture, but as a way for nuns to cross the street without interacting with the people around them. They lived cloistered lives, separated from the community. The arch allowed them to avoid contact with anyone outside their walls.

> *What barriers are keeping us from the people God placed in our path?*

I remember standing there, staring at that arch, thinking, "How many arches have we built in our own lives? How often do we separate ourselves from the very people we're called to love and serve?" The nuns believed they were protecting their holiness. But in doing so, they missed the holiness of connection. They missed being with people, sharing life, and recognizing the image of God in others.

That story shook me. It made me reevaluate how I viewed ministry, church, and even my own life.

What arches have we built?

What barriers are keeping us from the people God placed in our path?

FROM FILLING SEATS TO MEETING NEEDS

For years, I wrestled with what it meant to lead a church that truly lived out the Kingdom. Everything revolved around Sundays. All our time, budget, and energy went into the Sunday morning worship service. But deep down, I knew there had to be more.

We launched a second campus in 2018, thinking it would make a bigger impact in our city. It didn't.

By 2019, we were burned out. We were doing all the "right" things but not seeing the transformation we longed for.

When COVID hit in 2020, everything stopped. Honestly, I welcomed the break. I needed it. But when we slowly returned to in-person gatherings, something felt off. It wasn't just that things had changed. It was that they hadn't. Our first sermon series back was called "A New Normal." That lasted about six weeks before everything slid back into the old normal. I was tired of the cycle. I was tired of pouring everything into something that felt broken. I didn't want to walk away from Jesus, but I did consider walking away from organized church.

In 2021, during my sabbatical, I finally had space to evaluate everything. I needed to rediscover what church was supposed to be. Not just for Hill City, but for me. That led to a year of discovery.

The year 2022 was not a season of big moves or major decisions. It was a time of listening, reflecting, and being open to what God wanted to show me. So I waited, even if I wasn't good at it.

CHURCH REDEFINED: RELIFE

In 2023, everything began to come together. All those years of asking the same questions started to lead toward something tangible.

We had been asking:
- How do we live out the gospel beyond Sunday mornings?
- How do we reach people who may never walk through our doors?
- What does real community impact look like?

We wanted to be the kind of church that, if we closed our doors tomorrow, our city would actually notice. We didn't need more services. We needed a new model.

Then something clicked.

In February of that year, I called to make an offer on a property for my personal real estate portfolio. The realtor said, "We're only accepting offers from owner-occupants, government agencies, or non-profits."

And that's when it hit me.

We are a non-profit.

That was the beginning of what would become ReLife.

ReLife is a community-focused initiative that grew out of Hill City Church. It began with one simple shift: rethinking church through the lens of practical impact. We didn't need to reinvent the wheel. Our city already had incredible ministries. Our role was to meet the needs that were still being overlooked.

One of our partner organizations ran an eighteen-month program for single moms trying to rebuild their lives. But when the program ended, these women had nowhere to go. There were no affordable housing options. No next step. No support system.

That is where ReLife came in.

Our mission became clear. We would create family stability by providing affordable housing for single moms. Not just a roof, but a foundation. We began renovating homes and offering them at accessible rent through thoughtful investments and partnerships. Each house became more than a structure. It became a haven. A space to breathe, reset, and start again.

But ReLife is not just about housing. It is a culture. It is a commitment to walk with these women through mentorship, community, and support. It offers dignity instead of charity. Empowerment instead of dependency.

The most surprising part has been who is showing up. People who have never attended our church. People from other churches. People from other states. People with no connection to faith at all. Contractors, donors, volunteers, and city officials are linking arms with us because they believe in what is happening.

And what is happening is simple. Church is being redefined.

This is what it looks like to move from filling seats to meeting needs.

We now have a full ReLife Committee that oversees projects and logistics. We have a property manager, a project manager, and a ministry liaison who nurtures partnerships with other local organizations. Every woman is matched with a mentor who walks with her through the journey. And that is just the beginning.

One of the properties we acquired included an old church building. We didn't turn it into another worship venue. Instead, it is becoming a community center. It will host resume-writing classes, entrepreneurship workshops, therapy groups, and trauma support meetings. It will also serve as our ReLife HQ. It may not look like a church, but it is where the Church comes alive.

The most unexpected transformation has happened in the neighborhoods themselves. We thought we were renovating homes. Instead, we are helping rebuild trust on entire streets.

This is what happens when we stop asking, "How do we grow the church?" and start asking, "How do we love our city well?" This is what it looks like to move from filling seats to meeting needs.

And maybe this is what the future looks like.

I hope ReLife helps you ask better questions. Not "How do we get people to come?" but "What if they never do?"

What kind of love stays anyway?

What kind of impact leaves the fingerprints of Jesus without quoting a single verse?

What kind of church would your city miss if it disappeared?

That is the one I want to help build.

THE STOVE: A KINGDOM MOMENT

During the renovation of our second ReLife home, I met Teresa, the next-door neighbor everyone warned me about. They said to stay away. They believed she was selling drugs. One day, I started a conversation with her. She invited me in and started telling me about her family and her situation. I learned her stove had been broken for months. She was struggling to cook meals.

Without thinking, I told her, "God loves you, and He's going to get you a stove." I didn't know how that would happen, but I believed it. A couple of weeks later, I was walking through Home Depot. I figured I would just buy her one. That is when I ran into a guy who had visited our church recently.

We started talking, and he asked what I was doing. I told him about Teresa. He smiled and said, "You're not going to believe this. I have a stove in my truck right now. I was cleaning out a house and didn't know who to give it to."

When we love people with no agenda, heaven shows up right here on earth.

I couldn't believe it. God's provision was already parked outside.

When we delivered that stove, it was more than just an appliance. It was a statement. It was a reminder that God sees her. That she matters. That she is not forgotten. That she is loved.

Moments like that keep happening. They remind me that when we love people with no agenda, heaven shows up right here on earth.

COME OUTSIDE AND SEE THE STARS

There is a story in Genesis 15 where God speaks to Abram. Abram had been given a promise, but it had not come to pass. He began to question it. Then God did something unexpected.

Scripture says, "[The Lord] took him outside and said, 'Look up at the sky and count the stars—if indeed you can count them.' Then he said to him, 'So shall your offspring be'" (v. 5, NIV).

Why did God take Abram outside? Because he was inside his tent. He was staring at the ceiling. His view was limited. God wanted him to see more.

Outside the tent, the stars were visible. Countless. Limitless. And in that moment, Abram believed.

I believe God is still doing that today. He is calling us outside of our tents. He is calling us to step away from limited thinking, from safe structures, and from routines that no longer require faith.

The tent represents fear, control, and comfort. But the sky represents promise. The stars remind us how big God is and how deeply He cares.

Stepping outside is not just a physical act. It is a mindset shift. It is the willingness to let go of how things have always been and open ourselves to what God might be doing next.

We find His Kingdom in those ordinary, often messy places. In the stove given to a neighbor. In the house restored for a single mom. In a conversation on a front porch. In the open sky.

The reward is not in staying safe. It is in the journey. It is in saying yes. It is in looking up.

The stars are waiting.

CHAPTER 8

Carnage and Grace

Losing Everything to Find What Matters Most

By Tullian Tchividjian

The older I get, the more I realize how much my life is one long testament to this abiding truth. I'm not overstating things when I say that discovering the message of God's one-way love in all its radicality saved my marriage, my relationship with my kids, and my ministry. So this is not an abstract subject to me. One-way love is my lifeblood.

Those words were published in a best-selling book of mine called One Way Love,[24] back in

---
24 Tullian Tchividjian, *One Way Love: Inexhaustible Grace for an Exhausted World* (Colorado Springs, CO: David C. Cook, 2012).

2012—which, dear God, feels like a lifetime ago. I still stand by those words. But to say things got complicated after that is a gross understatement. I really had no idea. No, God's grace wasn't entirely abstract, but in that other, visceral sense, yes—it was. You see, grace doesn't really prevail until we run out of steam. And I hadn't yet arrived at the place where I was out of aces. I had yet to truly thirst for grace like that psalmic deer panting for water. I hadn't come to the end of me, with nothing else to hold on to, no one and nowhere else to turn.

I really had no idea.

USED TO BE ...

There's a certain amount of longing in that phrase, isn't there? It's almost always said with a sigh. Those words immediately set up a past-tense frame of mind—some things used to be a certain way for a time or a season, but they're not that way anymore. Things changed.

I know that phrase well.

I used to be an influential Christian leader, following in the footsteps of my famous grandfather, Billy Graham. I used to lead a large, famous church in my hometown of Fort Lauderdale—Coral Ridge Presbyterian Church. I used to write a book a year, and they used to be award-winning bestsellers. I used to travel extensively across the country—doing book tours, speaking at conferences, churches, universities, and various events. I used to be on TV every week around the globe, and on the radio every day. I used to be a popular guy, a widely sought-after guy, a "successful" guy. I used to have the world by the tail, as they say. I used to have it all—and then some. In a word, I used to be a winner. And man, it felt good.

But then things changed. *Used to be* imploded. Unraveled. Life as I knew it came crashing down. My sins caught up with me—they always do. That was the beginning of the learning years—minutes and hours and days and weeks and months of learning what it means to lose.

I used to consider two things to be secure forever and ever, amen: my twenty-one-year marriage and my role as a pastor. In 2015, I lost both. I cheated on my first wife and got caught. And because of my public persona, I lost both my marriage and my ministry (and everything else) in a very public way. If you pressed me for a reason behind it all, I'd have to point to that haunting phrase in Jimmy Buffett's "Margaritaville"[25]—my own damn fault.

But loss never happens in a vacuum. Those two monumental losses were the dominoes that tipped a thousand others:

The loss of peace and security on my kids' faces.
The loss of close friendships.
The loss of purpose.
The loss of public (and private) credibility.
The loss of influence.
The loss of confidence in God's friendship.
The loss of financial stability, of hope, of joy.

---

[25] Jimmy Buffett, vocalist, "Margaritaville" by Jimmy Buffett, 1997, track 6 on *Changes in Latitudes, Changes in Attitudes*, ABC.

The loss of opportunity.
The loss of life as I used to know it.
The loss of life as I used to *love* it.

And in addition to being the cause of my own losses, I caused loss in many other people's lives as well. First and foremost, I caused loss in the lives of those who depended on me as a husband, a father, and a spiritual leader—those who trusted me to love and protect them. I violated that trust. I betrayed their confidence. I injured their hearts. I devastated them.

And even though that happened over ten years ago, the consequences remain. There isn't a day that goes by when I'm not reminded in some way of what I did.

Cancelled and crushed overnight.

You can read about the fall in the headlines. It was everywhere. But what you won't read in those articles is the internal devastation.

What I didn't realize at the time was that a subtle shift had been taking place for years—a shift that came on like the slow creep of the tide, not a sudden tidal wave. It was a shift in identity—from locating my identity in God's love for me to locating it in what I was making of myself: my accomplishments, my accolades, my success, my network.

In other words, my worth, my value, my deepest sense of who I was and what made me matter—my identity—was anchored in my status, my reputation, my position, who my friends were, my communication skills, my ability to lead, the praise I received, the opportunities I had, financial security, and so on. Basically, the way the world has and always will measure worth. And because of this, my losses didn't simply usher in grief and pain and shame and regret.

They ushered in a crippling identity crisis.

We typically don't know what it is we depend on to make life worth living until we lose it. So, without the things I'd relied on to make me feel valuable and important, I no longer knew who I was. It wasn't just that I lost everything—I lost myself. I hadn't just lost things. I lost *me*.

You want to know what hell feels like? It feels like being exiled from your own self.

When I was feeling the most lost and hopeless—at my absolute worst and most desperate—my friend Paul Zahl said something to me that I will never forget: "Tullian, the purpose behind the suffering you are going through is to kick you into a new freedom from false definitions of who you are."

I didn't understand the depths of Paul's statement in that moment. There was no way I could have. But I've learned. And I'm learning.

I've come to see that failure, for all its brutality, can be strangely liberating. It strips away illusions. It burns down the scaffolding. It exposes the false gods we've built altars to—like reputation, platform, influence, usefulness. It reminds us that we are not the sum total of our accomplishments or accolades. It reminds us that we're not ultimately defined by what we've done or failed to do, our struggles or our successes, our strengths or our weaknesses.

Who we truly are, at our core, in other words, has nothing to do with us.

> ## God only loves failures because that's all He has to work with.

You *are* defined by God's unconditional love and acceptance of you. What you do with your life does not define you. What Jesus did with His life for you—that's what defines you. You are beloved. You are forgiven. You are held. Even when you can't hold on, He's holding you.

That is the Christian gospel. And that is freedom.

So, if you're reading this and you feel like a spiritual screw-up, take heart. God only loves and uses weak people who fail—because there aren't any other kinds of people. Let me say that again for the people in the back: God only loves failures because that's all He has to work with.

Your disqualifications don't disqualify you—they're your credentials. The only people who qualify for grace are the ones who admit they don't.

I'm now deeply embedded in the recovery community. Not because I had a substance addiction in the traditional sense, but because when you fall hard, you land in a room full of desperate people who know what it's like to be stripped bare.

And I've discovered that the recovery community often understands truth and grace better than the religious one. There's less pretense. More honesty. Less posturing. More vulnerability. Less blaming. More owning.

I've sat in circles with broken men and women who've told the truth about their lives—horrible truths, heartbreaking truths—and yet experienced something sacred in the sharing. I've found Jesus more often in those raw moments than in any church meeting I've ever been part of.

I've sat under brilliant minds—PhDs in theology, church history, New Testament, Old Testament. And I'm grateful. I learned a lot from these well-educated people. But I've learned more about sin and grace and forgiveness from people in active recovery than in any classroom. I've heard more truth in the trembling voice of an addict admitting powerlessness than in a thousand polished sermons. More self-awareness in rehab than in most churches. More honesty in raw confessions than in buttoned-up testimonies. Redemption has a face—and it looks a lot like a felon, an adulterer, a divorcée, a drunk finally getting honest.

God's not limited to religious spaces or sacred words. He speaks through the wrecked and the weary, the messed-up and the misunderstood. He's preaching through people who don't even know they're preaching—accidental saints, wounded healers. People like me. People like you.

Yes, I've found God in all the wrong places—the places they swore He'd never go. In my brokenness, my desperation, my infidelity. In suicidal thoughts, hopeless nights, guilty mornings, and shame-soaked regrets. In my badness, my rebellion, my arrogance, my recklessness.

He met me there. Not in my strength, but in my collapse. Not in my virtue, but in my vice.

And He didn't just show up in unlikely places—I've heard Him speak through the most unlikely people. The ones they said weren't qualified:

Alcoholics.

Divorced dads.

Unfaithful wives.

Porn addicts.

Chain smokers.

People with track marks and rap sheets.

Random people at the gym.

People who don't fit the mold, who don't speak the lingo, who don't check the boxes.

He keeps crashing into my life through breakups and breakdowns—in the real stuff, the raw stuff, the hard stuff, the bad stuff. As Leonard Cohen said, "There is a crack in everything. That's how the light gets in."[26]

We were taught to look for "the light" in the sanctified places and to listen for "the light" through the sanctified

---

26 Leonard Cohen, vocalist, "Anthem" by Leonard Cohen, November 24, 1992, track 5 on *The Future*, Columbia Records.

people. But God keeps showing up in the cracked ones—in the ordinary, the overlooked, the secular. So, if you've missed Him in the religious settings, don't worry.

> *My darkest exile became the brightest grace.*

He's not lost. He's just not confined to the places, or the voices, they told us He'd be.

Ten years later... after the crash, the burn, the fallout, facing the bloodbath I caused, and the long road of amend-making and recovery, I can honestly say this: Getting canceled by the Christian subculture was the best thing that could've happened to me.

My darkest exile became the brightest grace.

In the wreckage, I found freedom. I found people who bleed out loud, who tell the truth about themselves even when it's ugly. Outside the sanitized bubble of Christian subculture, I met the misfits, the addicts, the failures—those with dirt under their nails and failure on their résumé.

And they are real. Raw. Honest. Unimpressed by religious performance, allergic to fakeness and pious platitudes. These are my people now. And I'm never going back.

I may have lost my place in the system, but I found my soul.

I'm not where I thought I'd be at this stage of life. I'm not leading a big church. I'm not writing bestsellers. I'm not flying first class to speak to thousands. I don't have the influence I used to.

And honestly? I'm good with that. Because something else has happened.

The people closest to me say I'm less and more than I used to be. I'm less "what's next?" and more present. Less Superman (thank God) and more humane. Less self-assured and more self-aware. Less larger-than-life and more down-to-earth. Softer than I used to be—they say more understanding, more empathetic.

My own failures have forced me to reckon with God's forgiveness in a way that's made me more forgiving without even trying. As a result, I'm less likely to hold a grudge. I'm far more grateful for the smaller things now. You could say that small things are a big deal to me these days. I take a lot less for granted. People matter more—way more. Projects matter less—way less.

I'm more of a friend and less of a networker. I enjoy listening more. I love the things that matter most, more. Minutes and moments are so much more important to me now. I care way more about today and much less about tomorrow.

Life is smaller and slower than it used to be. A lot smaller. And much slower. And I love it.

It's less grand, less busy, less impressive. I have less stuff, less money, fewer connections. I'm less celebrated, less influential, and less sought-after. And yet, I couldn't care less about all that these days.

Because life is slower and smaller, I see more, hear more, feel more. Things are quieter inside me. I'm less distracted. I'm way more content, way more free, and way more comfortable in my own skin.

Have I arrived? Ha! That's funny. No—not by a long shot.

These days, I live with a seemingly incurable low-grade fever of sadness because of the people I hurt and some of the relationships I lost. It's the grievous wound of *used to be* that won't heal. I live with lopped-off limbs. I still feel like I'm white-knuckling it some days—prone to wander, taking destructive detours in my heart. Yes, I'm fully aware of my capacity to screw it all up again, repeating my adulterous history.

Lord, have mercy.

But some place or picture of *arrival* is not what I'm grasping after. If I'm reaching at all, it's to receive what's been so graciously given: Stacie's love. A family of screwed-up, misfit friends. The voices of my children and grandchildren. Sunsets and ocean breezes. Midnight music festivals with my daughter under the Miami night sky.

I think those who know me best would say I've found some measure of peace and contentment in acceptance. That as I make my living amends, there's a lightness about me. I can sing again. I've got a laughing heart. One with no reason to pretend anymore. One that only comes by learning to relax the way we relax in the presence of someone we're certain is fond of us. One that dances to the tune of endless grace—the grace that never ceases to comfort me throughout my carnage-riddled life. A laughing heart has only one beat: Gratitude.

Poet Maya Popa captures this sentiment perfectly in the title of her book: *Wound is the Origin of Wonder*.[27] That it is. And I'm grateful for the wonder that now marks my wounded, rattletrap life.

Frederick Buechner famously wrote: "*Here is the world. Beautiful and terrible things will happen. Don't be afraid.*"[28] That's the abundant life, my friends—experiencing the abundance. All of it. The beautiful and the terrible and everything in between. Every stitch. Right in the *cardia*.

Grace, always grace.[29]

---

27 Maya C. Popa, *Wound is the Origin of Wonder: Poems* (New York, NY: W. W. Norton & Company, 2022).
28 Frederick Buechner, *Beyond Words: Daily Readings in the ABC's of Faith* (New York, NY: Harper One, 2009).
29 Full chapter adapted from Tullian Tchividjian, *Carnage & Grace: Confessions of an Adulterous Heart* (Brenham, TX: Lucid Books, 2024).

CHAPTER 9

Love Without Leashes

When Letting Go Sets Everyone Free

By Joyce de Vos

*Y*ears ago, as a growing girl, I had an idealistic vision: the whole world had to—and would—become friends with one another. Only then would everything be better, more beautiful, and more loving. And how hard could it be? Surely that is what God had intended? I think, somewhere deep inside, I knew I had been given an unspoken life mission. And this little girl was going to give it her all.

When I read the Bible and held it up against my secret mission, everything seemed to line up. So many verses about love jumped out at me. I highlighted them one by one, and as a result, my Bible practically exploded with yellow markings. This *had* to be it. I had discovered it. The world just needed to understand....

Shortly after I married David, I wrote my first book, *Unconditional*. Indirectly, it was my plea for world peace—one that, in my mind, could break through at any moment. I challenged my readers to view the people around them through a different lens: the lens of unconditional love. My hope was that this would inspire them to let go of disagreements and conflicts and simply love one another. I thought it was a gap in the market. After all, who else was writing about this?

During that same period, I took several personality tests. Every result confirmed what I already knew: I'm a people person with a team spirit; someone who prefers harmony over conflict. I scored sky-high in that area. As soon as tension arose, I felt uncomfortable, and my mind would automatically switch to solution mode. Because for me, harmony was sacred.

For years, I held on tightly to that secret mission. I started writing songs, published blogs all about love and relatability, and was invited to speak here and there. Wherever I went, love and unity always took center stage. Because if people could *really* understand . . . everything would be okay. Right?

My heart and motivations are still the same, but certain events have permanently and drastically changed my view of unconditional love over the past five years. In this chapter, I'll take you on that journey.

CONFRONTATIONS IN A DIVIDED WORLD

In 2020, the COVID era began—a time when friendships, marriages, families, and churches came under pressure. When our organization *Go and Tell* hosted our annual *Simply Jesus* event, we were hit with some of the most painful accusations. The event was only accessible to those who were vaccinated or could present a test. Many Christians felt excluded—or even betrayed. I'll never forget how uncomfortable I felt, especially within my own familiar Christian bubble.

> *Putting relationships above opinions isn't always easy, but I believe God calls us to do just that—especially when we disagree.*

And that wasn't the only storm. Tension erupted within my own family and circle of friends. We turned out to have fundamentally different views on these kinds of topics. In our attempts to understand each other—the more you love someone, the stronger that desire—the more effort we made to explain our perspectives. But no matter how good the intentions were, it created distance. And that hurt—on both sides.

Agreeing to disagree and still remaining good friends? For many—especially in the Netherlands—that's a bridge too far. If you have a different opinion, it's often shouted from the rooftops. And I get that urge. At home, I want my men to always agree with me, too. But it doesn't always work out like that. We're made differently, so we think differently. Sometimes it's complicated—but that's just how it is. And if that's how it works in a single household, how much more so outside of it?

The challenges David and I faced during those years—both nationally and within our family—weren't just our story. They were the story of so many others. If it wasn't about COVID, it was about something else. The biggest challenge often isn't having different viewpoints, but how we deal with them. Putting relationships above opinions isn't always easy, but I believe God calls us to do just that—especially when we disagree.

How beautiful would it be if we focused on what we have in common instead of what divides us? That's what we as a family chose to do, right in the middle of all the COVID chaos. Our love turned out to be stronger than the differences in our convictions. I've come to accept that major disagreements can also bring feelings of grief. It is a kind of loss when people you love don't seem to be on "your side." But it doesn't have to be a barrier. In fact, it creates space to learn—to think beyond your own framework, and to love what is completely different from you.

A BOOK, A BREAK, AND THE STORM THAT FOLLOWED

After COVID, things quieted down. No more vaccines, no more masks, no more entry requirements. Looking back, it almost felt like a bad dream we had finally woken up from. For a moment I thought: maybe world peace really is still possible. Secretly, I felt a flicker of hope. But it didn't last long.

In September 2023, we celebrated David's 40th birthday, surrounded by his closest friends. I felt richer than ever. It felt like we were finally closing a heavy chapter. If you've read *Rauw* (Raw),[30] you know how much has happened in our private lives. Now there was room again to look forward. But what I didn't know then was that another hard year was waiting for us.

The biography *Rauw* was still in development when I read the manuscript for the first time. And to be honest? It was confronting. Reading back through our journey—the mental struggles, the conflicts—these were things I would have rather kept private. Now the whole world would read them. We wrestled with some parts quite a bit, but in the end, a manuscript emerged that we both fully stood behind.

When the *Algemeen Dagblad* published a critical article before the book even launched, when *Simply Jesus* was

---
30 Marcel Langedijk, *Raw: The Honest Story* (Go and Tell Media, 2024).

canceled by DoorBrekers, and when many Christians took issue with David's statement "Everyone is a child of God," something inside me broke. My harmony-seeking heart went into crisis again. I fell into a black hole. The shutters on our windows stayed closed for weeks. I even shopped outside of our town because I was afraid of being treated with hostility. Everything inside me was in turmoil.

Except our relationship. Precisely during this time, all the energy—and therapy—we had invested began to bear fruit. Years ago, we had emotionally lost sight of each other. But now we held on tightly. We understood each other's differences and encouraged each other to keep growing. That in itself was a miracle.

FROM CRISIS TO CREATION

To provide more context around the book, we took it on the road: twelve theater nights in twelve provinces. And I didn't want to miss a single one. Not only because of the content, but because of the conversations afterward. So many people were touched, enlightened, or even healed by *Rauw*'s[31] story. Some encountered God again—or for the very first time. After such a tough season, it felt like everything had meaning after all.

Meanwhile, David's statement, "Everyone is a child of God," continued to stir strong reactions. Psalm 139 is one of my favorite Bible passages. It says that God knit us together in our mother's womb. If that's true, why

---
31 Langedijk, *Raw*.

does that statement provoke so much resistance? What triggers Christians so deeply that they feel the need to express their outrage publicly—visible to outsiders? What kind of message are we sending to the world? I felt ashamed of my Christian bubble.

> *No one holds the exclusive rights to truth.*

David launched *Rauw Talks*—honest conversations about sensitive topics. The responses were predictable: resistance, harsh comments, donors withdrawing their support. I felt that familiar unease rise again. "Should we stop, David? Are we pushing too far?" I asked through tears. But the truth was, my unrest ran deeper. I just wanted everyone to like us. My greatest fear was losing our good reputation.

And yet—I began to understand our critics, too. I recognized that resistance in myself. I also protest when things go differently than I'd hoped or planned, especially when my certainties are shaken. More and more, I started to see their reactions as expressions of grief. Not as resistance toward *us*, but toward their own pain. And that brought me peace.

I also saw that David's drive to open up new perspectives wasn't about being a contrarian. His evangelistic heart was opening up even more. He longed to share the Good News with everyone: *You belong. No conditions. No achievements. Just receive it*—freely. I saw a burden lift off his shoulders. And it moved me deeply.

LOVE THAT'S GREATER THAN BEING RIGHT

With more than 45,000 church denominations worldwide, I came to a realization: no one holds the exclusive rights to truth. Maybe what we need most is to let go of the idea that we must have ultimate truths in order to stand firm. There must be room for questions, for doubts, for nuance—and for those who think differently. As David always says, "God doesn't fall off His throne when you doubt." And I believe that too. God isn't looking for our answers; He's looking for our hearts—so He can fill them with His love.

There are only a few moments in the Bible when God's voice is audibly heard. One of them is when He says, "You are my beloved Son; in You I am well pleased." If that's what God says about Jesus—and if we believe we are His children—shouldn't that be the core message to all of us? That we are loved, wanted, and seen? And that nothing can separate us from His love?

BREAK IN THE CHURCH, HEALING IN THE HEART

Just when I thought the storm had passed, another came. The church I had been part of for eighteen years went through a split. A painful one, with deep impact—on me, on neighbors in our village—no matter which side we were on.

I was involved in music leadership, but when things began to shift, I decided to return to my responsibilities. In the past, this would have completely shaken me internally, but this time I remained remarkably calm. Maybe because I've learned to trust that nothing happens without purpose.

With the time I suddenly had, I turned inward. I tried to organize my thoughts to process and, most of all, to rest. I picked up my songbook—the one I often traveled with. But nothing came. No melodies, no lyrics. Just a few scattered words and scribbles.

I had given up hope for new inspiration. Until, in the wake of the church crisis and during a season of complete rest, creativity began to flow again. While cooking. In the shower. In the car. Even in my sleep. All I needed was a voice recorder.

Before I knew it, ten new songs were born—without expectation. And that was surprising, because "having expectations" always seemed like a prerequisite before I could make things happen. But it was actually that **pause for breath** that brought me where I needed to be. Sometimes, the most beautiful things arise when you stop trying to force them. Have you ever experienced that?

FREEDOM IN LETTING GO

So what now, with all the divisions in the Church? I used to think everything had to be fixed. But here, too, my perspective has changed. Differences of opinion will always exist. Sometimes, people grow apart. It's painful, yes—but it doesn't mean you're stuck. You *can*—you *must*—move forward with your life. And in that process, it's crucial not to let bitterness take root. No matter what happens.

> *But more than ever, I find freedom in letting people go to be who they are, believe what they believe, and think how they think.*

The past five years have been intense, but full of learning. More than ever before, I see how God created us all differently. Where I highlighted verses about love and peace in my Bible, someone else highlights ones about battle and justice. Where my personality craves harmony, that's secondary for someone else. And that's a good thing. We need each other to stay balanced.

I now also see that the Bible is full of conflict. And conflict doesn't have to be the end. It can lead to depth, to growth. It reveals who you are—your strength *and* your vulnerability. Think of Abraham and Lot: after their conflict, their land expanded. Or Jacob and Esau: they both came out stronger. And what about Jesus Himself? By embracing conflict, He defeated death once and for all!

And yes, love and unity are still my blueprint. God put that in me. I want to build bridges. Create connection. Foster understanding. But more than ever, I find freedom in letting people go to be who they are, believe what they believe, and think how they think. That too is love. That too is following the way of Jesus: the man without judgment. The man who only ever got angry at those who blocked the way to His Father.

My definition of love has widened. It's more than a character trait. Love *is* God. And Love always wins.

CHAPTER 10

Love's Final "No" and Forever "Yes"

From Adam's Fall to the Father's Embrace

By Dr. C. Baxter Kruger

Why did Jesus die? Why was his death necessary? What happened in his death, and what does it mean for us? In every sphere of life—relationships, science, and Christian faith—we must seek to know things as they truly are. Without understanding the dynamics behind an event like Jesus's death, we risk misinterpretation. We must uncover what made his death necessary and grasp its context. Otherwise, we're left with a "fake" Jesus—uninspiring and incapable of producing true life and passion. Clarity isn't a luxury; it's life or death.

Two great realities form the true context of Christ's death. The first is the heart of God—both His purpose for us and the fire in His belly to see that purpose fulfilled at any cost.

The death of Jesus Christ is part of a seamless movement that began in eternity with the Father, Son, and Spirit, culminating in the exaltation of humanity through Jesus's ascension to the right hand of the Father. To understand why Jesus died, we must return to the eternal decision of the Trinity to include us in Their shared life. What drives Jesus to the cross is the Father's relentless passion to have us as His beloved children. Jesus died because God loves us with an unshakable, everlasting love that refuses to let us perish. The second great reason for His death is what the Bible calls "sin"—the profound spiritual disease that entered through Adam and threatened creation itself. Jesus died because the Father would not abandon His dream for us, and the only way to fulfill that dream, in light of sin, was to recreate humanity through death and resurrection.

THE FIRE IN GOD'S BELLY

What sets the Christian vision of God apart from other religions? Two unparalleled truths: the doctrine of the Trinity and the humility of God. Unlike the distant, self-absorbed gods of human imagination—distant, unapproachable, and preoccupied with themselves and with things far more important than human existence—the Christian God stoops, entering human history in the most personal way. He desires union with us and is willing to humble Himself, even suffer, to make it possible. Other gods remain aloof, concerned with their own glory, but the God of Christianity draws near.

> *From the start, His plan has been to give us nothing less than Himself.*

The Christian God is the opposite of the self-centered gods of human imagination. He is not a taker, but a giver—one who despises being untouchable. From before the beginning, God has had staggering plans for us. He is not indifferent or distant, but deeply invested in our welfare, determined to bless us with life, fullness, and glory. The Christian God eagerly crosses the infinite chasm between Creator and creature to lift us up into union with Himself. This vision is unique—a God of grace, humility, and other-centeredness, who doesn't just seek relationship, but union, and not just union, but full participation in His own joy, beauty, and divine life. From the start, His plan has been to give us nothing less than Himself.

Part of what John means when he says Jesus Christ is the Word of God (John 1:1, 14) is that there has never been a moment in eternity when God wanted to be without us. Jesus—the incarnate Son, the humanity of God—is not an afterthought or an afterword. He is the eternal foreword. The relationship between God and humanity forged in Jesus Christ is not a backup plan; it is the eternal plan of God, preceding creation itself. God has always purposed to become flesh. This is His eternal Word, spoken from His very being as the God who loves and is determined to bless us beyond all we can imagine. "Not God alone, but God and man together constitute the content of the Word of God attested in Scripture."[32]

Behind this vision of God stooping to enter into relationship, into union, with human beings in order to bless us, is the fact that God is Father, Son, and Spirit. The Bible tells us that the Father *loves* the Son and that the Son *loves* the Father and that they share all things in the love and unchained *fellowship* of the Spirit. Nothing that could be said about God is more fundamental than this mutual love and this fellowship. God exists as Father, Son, and Spirit in a rich and glorious and overflowing fellowship of acceptance and delight and passion and love. The dream of human existence begins right here in the unstifled fellowship and togetherness of the Father, Son, and Spirit.

Everything we say about God—His love, holiness, righteousness, fullness, and joy—is ultimately a reflection of the relationship between the Father, Son, and Spirit. To believe in the Trinity is to believe that God is, and always has been, a relational being. Fellowship,

---
32 Karl Barth, *Church Dogmatics* (Edinburgh: T. & T. Clark, 1956), Vol. I/2, p. 207.

togetherness, self-giving, and other-centeredness aren't add-ons to God's nature—they are the essence of who He is. The Father is not self-consumed; He loves the Son and the Spirit. The Son is not riddled with narcissism; He delights in the Father and the Spirit. The Spirit is not preoccupied with His own glory; He loves the Father and the Son. Giving, not taking—sharing, not hoarding—lies at the very center of God's life. This is the beauty of the Trinity: a God whose wholeness is found in relationship, not isolation.

When Christianity says God, it says relationship—self-giving love expressed in boundless fellowship and joyous unity. It does not say self-centered, distant, detached, indifferent, or austere. It does not say lonely, sad, bored, or in need. Christianity says Father, Son, and Spirit in a relationship of delight, acceptance, and overflowing love—a relationship so rich and real, so open and good, that we can only say God is three, yet utterly one. Though eternally distinct, their love is so pure and their fellowship so deep that any word short of "one" falls short of describing their togetherness.

Such is the Christian vision of God—but we dare not stop there. The moment we speak of the Triune relationship, we've said something profound about the entire cosmos. This joyous fellowship, this unspeakable oneness of love, is the very womb of the universe and of humanity within it.

The universe, our solar system, the earth, and humanity are not eternal. There was a time when they were not—when only the circle of the Holy Trinity existed. Creation—the birth of all things, seen and unseen—was the act of the Triune God. Paul tells us this creative act followed a prior decision (Ephesians 1:4-5): it was the fruit of purpose, the overflow of a determined heart.

Before the blueprints of creation were drawn, the Father, Son, and Spirit set their love and abundant grace upon us. God did not hoard the Trinitarian life and glory but chose to share it, to lavish it upon us. Why? Because at the center of everything is the deep, abiding love of the Triune God. That circle of mutual delight, intimacy, and eternal wholeness is the source and goal of all divine thought and activity.

Why is God this way? Why would the Father, Son, and Spirit set the fullness of their love and lavish grace upon us, determining such a glorious destiny? The only answer lies in the mutual love of the Trinity. In one way or another, the existence of everything—especially every human being—finds its purpose in the deep, abiding love of the Triune God. That circle of love, intimacy, fellowship, mutual delight, and eternal wholeness is the matrix, the roux, of all divine thought and activity.

> *Jesus died because the Triune God absolutely refused to abandon their dream for us.*

The impulse to share, to include, to bless—along with the unwavering determination to do so at any cost—flows directly from the relationship of the Father, Son, and Spirit. Such extravagant philanthropy, other-centeredness, and sacrificial care are not exceptions for God; they are the way God is. This is the truest truth about God, the deepest part of the divine well.

But why this love is turned toward us—why we are the recipients—is another question. It is consistent with who God is, but not required. There is no necessity in it, only grace. And before such love, we can only stand amazed, astonished, and thrilled.

Christian faith begins with such astonishment.

This decision—flowing from the very being of God—to share all that the Father, Son, and Spirit are and have with us, and the relentless determination that it would be so, is the true context for the death of Jesus Christ. Jesus died because the Triune God absolutely refused to abandon their dream for us. "For God so loved the world," Jesus says, "that He gave His only Son…" (John 3:16, ESV). Before creation, God had already determined to include humanity in the Trinitarian circle of life, fullness, and joy. And with that decision came a fire in God's belly to see it through, no matter the cost. The Lamb was slain before the foundation of the world.

So what did God do when Adam fell into sin? Did He walk away in disgust, explode with anger, or plot vengeance? No. The Fall was met by the eternal Word of God. The chaos and ruin of Adam's rebellion were met with a fierce divine "No! I did not create you to perish. I did not create you to flounder in misery, to live in such appalling pain and brokenness and heartache and destitution. I created you for life, to share in My life and glory, to participate in the fullness and joy, the free-flowing fellowship and goodness and wholeness that I share with My Son and Spirit. And I will have it no other way. It will be so."

Over forty times, John tells us in his gospel that Jesus Christ was *sent* by God the Father. John saw that the coming of Jesus Christ, his death on the cross, flowed out of the endless love of the Father for us and out of His unyielding determination that His purpose for us would be fulfilled.

The death of Jesus Christ is the revelation of the fact that the Father has never abandoned us, never forsaken us, that He refuses to go back on his dream to include us in the circle of life. Jesus's death is part of the fulfillment of the eternal purpose of God, part of a seamless movement designed to lay hold of the human race and lift us up into the Trinitarian life of God. For the Father will have it no other way. He will be "satisfied" with nothing less.

THE FALL OF ADAM AND THE DIVINE DILEMMA

To understand the death of Jesus Christ, we must begin in eternity with the Father, Son, and Spirit—and with their decision to include humanity in their shared life and glory. This decision forms the foundation for the incarnation, life, death, resurrection, and ascension of Jesus. He became human to create an everlasting relationship between his Father and the human race, to be the mediator through whom divine life intersects human existence, lifting us into the Trinitarian circle. Without this eternal purpose, there would be no creation, incarnation, or cross.

The fire in God's belly—His relentless love—drives both the incarnation and the death of Christ. But within this larger story is another crucial truth: the only path from the catastrophe of Adam to the right hand of the Father is through death. The Fall was so devastating that to redeem us required nothing less than recreation through death and resurrection.

Growing up, I learned the *Westminster Shorter Catechism's* legal definition: "Sin is any want of conformity unto, or transgression of, the law of God."[33] But sin runs deeper than lawbreaking. The real problem is disease—a spiritual cancer. The legal framework confuses the fruit with the root. Sin corrupts our very being.

In college, I came across Athanasius's *On the Incarnation of the Word of God*, a book that unexpectedly shaped my understanding. Athanasius insisted it was unthinkable for God to turn His back on the creation He loved. When faced with humanity's ruin, Athanasius asked: *What was God, being good, to do when His creation*

---

[33] Westminster Assembly, *The Westminster Shorter Catechism: With Scripture Proofs* (Philadelphia: Presbyterian Board of Publication, 1852), Q.14.

was lapsing into non-being? His answer: the same divine determination to bless that birthed creation sent the Son to save it.[34]

Athanasius also taught me that sin is an organic problem. God's solution wasn't balancing a heavenly ledger—it was healing the disease. Forgiveness had to take root in real, embodied reconciliation that restored relationship. A few months later, preparing a Bible study, I reached for a visual aid: a bowl of rotten oranges, slimy and collapsing in on themselves. Sin, I told the group, is not merely doing wrong—it's corruption, alienation, a breakdown of our humanity from the inside out.

If God's purpose is to lift us into Trinitarian life, the disease must be healed. The cancer must be cut out—without losing us in the process. That is the challenge the love of the Trinity faced in the Fall.

The orange analogy is helpful but limited. To go deeper, we must look inside Adam's soul. Sin baptized him in anxiety. He and Eve were not just alive; they were filled with *abounding life*—the fullness that comes from being free to love and be loved, to know and be known, to give and receive. In true fellowship, something beyond us is awakened—something only possible through the freedom of God.

As my friend Cary Stockett says, this freedom wasn't "built in at the factory." It belonged to the Father, Son, and Spirit—and Adam and Eve shared in it. How?

---

[34] Athanasius of Alexandria, *On the Incarnation of the Word of God*, trans. and ed. a Religious of C.S.M.V. (London: A. R. Mowbray & Co., 1920), §6.

Through truth. Jesus said, "You will know the truth, and the truth will set you free" (John 8:31-32, NIV). In knowing the truth, they shared in God's freedom from self-centeredness, a freedom for self-giving and fellowship. And in that fellowship, their existence was filled with abounding life.

Adam and Eve belonged to God. They were His prized creation, the objects of His delight and breathtaking blessing. Living in the truth of who they were and to whom they belonged filled them with deep peace and abiding security. That assurance became the most powerful force in their lives—it gave them the freedom to love and be loved, to give and receive, to know and be known. From that freedom came fellowship, and from fellowship came *abounding life*—a life alive with joy, intimacy, and wholeness.

But all of it unraveled the moment they believed the serpent's lie. The Fall began not with the bite, but with the breach of trust—when they stopped believing the truth and accepted the illusion that God was holding out on them. Fear sliced through their souls like a razor. The assurance that once anchored them gave way to anxiety, insecurity, and guilt. The baptism of fear rewired their perception of God and each other. Hiding, self-protection, and self-centeredness followed, killing the freedom needed for fellowship and life.

Like a little girl paralyzed by belief in a monster in the closet, Adam and Eve were overwhelmed by a false narrative. The lie destroyed their joy and ushered in a cascade of sorrow—bitterness, envy, strife, even murder. Anxiety became the matrix of human existence, the poisonous roux saturating every part of creation.

Though they still drew breath, Adam and Eve no longer lived in the fullness they were made for. The lie they believed didn't just fracture their experience—it corrupted their very being. As Athanasius wrote, they began to lapse back into non-being. Alienated from God and cut off from His life, they teetered on the edge of annihilation. The Fall was not merely moral failure; it was existential collapse. And nothing less than divine intervention could restore what had been lost.

The deepest problem of sin wasn't simply that Adam and Eve disobeyed—it was that God's very presence, once their joy, now filled them with dread. "They hid themselves from the presence of the Lord" (Genesis 3:8, BSB). Why? Not because they feared punishment, but because perfect love now exposed their emptiness. The joy, freedom, and goodness of God became unbearable in contrast to their brokenness.

> ## God speaks in love, but we hear through distortion.

C.S. Lewis, in *The Great Divorce*, describes encountering a heavenly being whose presence felt like "a burden of solid gold."³⁵ It wasn't terror that crushed him—it was the weight of unfiltered goodness revealing his own unreality. That's what Adam and Eve feared. And so they hid. We've been hiding ever since.

But the tragedy goes deeper. The Fall didn't just sever fellowship—it warped perception. Adam and Eve began seeing God through new "mental glasses"—lenses shaped by anxiety, shame, and fear. God hadn't changed; He was still faithful, loving, and generous. But their view of Him had. They projected their brokenness onto His face, imagining a god who was temperamental, distant, and ready to reject.

This is the great dilemma of the Fall: a profound communication breakdown. God speaks in love, but we hear through distortion. His self-giving nature is misread as conditional. His fellowship feels like judgment. The fallen mind, wearing these mental glasses, interprets even divine grace as threat. The question remains: how can God pierce through our projections and reveal who He truly is?

ISRAEL AS THE WOMB OF THE INCARNATION

The response of the Father, Son, and Spirit to Adam's plunge into ruin can be summed up in one word: "No!" That "No" echoes the eternal "Yes" of God's will to share divine life with humanity. God is for us—and therefore utterly and passionately opposed to our destruction.

---

35 C. S. Lewis, *The Great Divorce* (New York: Collier Books, Macmillan Publishing Co., 1946) p. 64.

This is the proper understanding of the wrath of God: not the opposite of love, but love in opposing action.

From this opposition, the plan of reconciliation begins. God calls Abraham, forms a nation, and begins a long, painful relationship with Israel—not to dispense theology, but to draw near to fallen Adam in living fellowship. The law, given through Moses, was not the point. The point was contact—God re-entering into relationship with humanity.

One of T. F. Torrance's great contributions to Christian thought is the way he understands the gut-wrench of Israel's existence.[36] While Adam and Eve hid from God, Israel was called into direct fellowship with Him—not with abstract law, but with the living God. On one side was the unbounded joy and intimacy of the Father, Son, and Spirit; on the other, fallen and fearful Israel, projecting its brokenness onto God. How could such a relationship even be possible?

Again and again, Israel tried to run. The love and glory of God were simply too much to bear. Like Adam and Eve, they hid—building religion to keep God at a distance, imitating the nations around them. But God wouldn't let them go. Here was a people from Adam's fallen world, terrified and estranged, thrown into direct relationship with God Himself. Think again of C. S. Lewis's statement: "Here was an enthroned and shining god,

---

36 See *The Mediation of Christ* (Grand Rapids: Eerdmann, 1983), *God and Rationality* (London: Oxford University Press, 1971, Chapter 6: "The Word of God and the Response of Man," "Salvation of the Jews" [EQ vol. 22 (1950) pp. 164-13] and "Israel and the Incarnation" [Judica vol. 13 (1957) pp. 1-18].

whose ageless spirit weighed upon mine like a burden of solid gold."[37] Israel wasn't grappling with abstract ideas, but with a divine presence that invaded their reality and pressed on them as the burden of all burdens.

The painful ordeal of God's relationship with fallen Israel produced two key outcomes. First, it created a bridgehead into the estranged human mind. Through the Spirit's creative work, God's revelation began to penetrate Israel's projections and distortions, acting as a refining fire. The living Word wrestled with their fallen thinking and began clothing itself in human ideas. The fruit of such wrestling and conflict was the forging of new concepts and ideas such as covenant, faithfulness, sin, atonement, mercy, community, and prophet, priest and king, all of which would become "the essential furniture of our knowledge of God," as Torrance puts it.[38] These concepts, forged in the fire of revelation within Israel's fallen mind, became the new mental instruments—the glasses through which the world could begin to see God rightly and enter meaningful fellowship with the Father.

Second, the real presence of God in fallen Israel stirred a conflict that became the matrix of the incarnation. In Israel, the Word of God was already "on the road to becoming flesh,"[39] as Torrance says. Revelation wasn't abstract truth but the unveiling of God

---

37 Lewis, *The Great Divorce*.
38 Thomas F. Torrance, *The Mediation of Christ* (Grand Rapids: Eerdmans, 1983, p. 20.
39 T.F. Torrance, *Conflict and Agreement in the Church* (London: Lutterworth Press, 1959) vol. 1, 266.

Himself—a living encounter pressing toward embodiment. The Word longed not just to speak, but to dwell in flesh and blood.

This encounter exposed Israel's brokenness, refusing denial or hiding. It brought the Fall to the surface and sparked a profound struggle—the prehistory of atonement. In this tension, Israel—alienated and afraid—was summoned into real fellowship with the living God, setting the stage for the impossible union of God and fallen humanity.

The contradiction and the fellowship created by the revelation of God to Israel in her darkness and alienation constitute the first form of death and resurrection; the first hint of the end and the new beginning of fallen Adamic existence, of the new covenant, of Pentecost, and the coming of the Kingdom of God. But more than this, the conflict created by the unveiling of God to fallen Israel establishes the womb of the incarnation itself,[40] the living situation, the unbearable and agonizing tension into which the Son of God Himself would be born.

THE CONVERSION OF ADAMIC EXISTENCE IN JESUS CHRIST

To consider the ascension of Jesus Christ is to stand before the miracle of reconciliation. A son of Adam, a Jew, now sits face-to-face with the Father in unbroken

---

[40] The phrase is adapted from T.F. Torrance. See *God and Rationality* (London: Oxford University Press, 1971), 149; *Reality and Evangelical Theology* (Philadelphia: Westminster Press, 1982), 87 and *Theology in Reconstruction*, Chapter 8: "The Place of Christology in Biblical and Dogmatic Theology" (Grand Rapids: Wm B. Eerdmands Pub. Co., 1985), 145.

fellowship. This is the undoing of Eden's hiding and Israel's flight. Jesus's ascension proclaims that Adamic existence has been reordered, God and Israel reconciled, and the lie of the evil one crushed. Fellowship, not fear, now defines the covenant.

The Christian confession is not of a generic divine being, but of the Son—the eternal beloved of the Father—who, in the Spirit, stepped into our world. The incarnation is not God at a distance, but the full fellowship of the Trinity setting up shop inside Adamic flesh. Jesus did not leave behind the Trinity to become human; He brought it with Him into the quagmire of our estrangement.

This means that the Son of God entered not just human life, but fallen life. He saw what Adam saw. He put on Adam's mental glasses—those that distorted the Father's face into judgment and rejection—and He felt the weight of that illusion. Yet, without ever ceasing to be the faithful Son, He entered into the heart of our brokenness to redeem it from within.

The incarnation is the paradox of the eternal Son living inside Adamic alienation without surrendering His identity. For this contradiction to be resolved, either the Trinity must fracture—or Adam must be converted. The Triune fellowship didn't break. It went to war.

Jesus entered our shoes and refused to live fallen. Step by step, blow by blow, He bent back the twisted logic of the Adamic mind. His life was one long cruciform struggle—thirty-three years of faithfulness inside our estranged existence. Gethsemane was not the beginning of His suffering; it was a window into it.

On the cross, Jesus walked into the abyss of Adam's alienation. There, where the mythological god reigned in Adam's imagination, Jesus felt forsaken. "My God, My God, why have You forsaken Me?" (Matthew 27:46, ESV) was not the end, but the turning point. The final word was, "Father, into Your hands I commend My Spirit" (Luke 23:46, ESV). Even there, Jesus remained the Son—and the Trinity triumphed.

What emerged on the other side of the cross was a man—from Adam's world—who knows and loves the Father. A man in whom no trace of the Fall remains. In Jesus Christ, Adamic existence came to an end—and a new beginning.

The death of Jesus Christ was not divine punishment, but the Son's final "No!" to Adam's lie and His triumphant "Yes!" to the Father. It was the radical circumcision of Adamic flesh, the turning of estrangement into union, the triumph of fellowship over fear. Jesus is not a tool or a ledger-balancer. He is reconciliation itself—living, breathing atonement. The man from Adam's world now lives forever in the embrace of the Father, seated in the fellowship of the Spirit.

Why did Jesus die? Because the Triune God absolutely refuses to let us be destroyed. Because the only way from the Fall to the right hand of God was through the re-creation of Adamic existence—through incarnation, suffering, and the crucifixion of everything that separated us from the life of God.

THE GOOD NEWS

Even with the death, resurrection, and ascension of Jesus, we haven't yet reached the heart of the gospel. If we stop there, we're still spectators—watching from the outside. Yes, Adamic existence has been converted in Christ, but the Triune God's eternal purpose isn't complete until *we* are included.

The New Testament doesn't leave us contemplating Christ from afar. It declares that we were crucified with Him, raised with Him, and seated with Him at the Father's right hand. Paul puts it plainly in 2 Corinthians 5:14 (BSB): *"One died for all, therefore all died."* Somehow, in this one man, Jesus Christ, the whole human race was gathered up and carried through death to resurrection.

Scripture hints at this kind of representative connection—like the High Priest in the holy of holies, David fighting Goliath for all Israel, or Adam whose fall affected all humanity. These figures foreshadow the greater reality: Jesus, the true Head of the human race. Paul calls Adam a type of Christ (Romans 5:14), but Christ is the substance.

The gospel rests on this foundational truth: an objective union between Jesus Christ and the human race. In Him, we were implicated. What happened to Christ happened to us. Our identity, history, and relationship with God were fundamentally reordered in Him. The

New Testament tells us what became of the Son of God because it wants us to see what became of us in Him.

Without this connection—without *"one died for all, therefore all died"*—there is no good news. But because of it, the gospel is nothing less than the proclamation that in Christ, humanity has been crucified, buried, and raised into new life.

Paul saw it: in Jesus Christ, Adam's fall, sin, and alienation—ours included—were brought to an end. All of it was put to death. And then came the resurrection. If we died with Christ, what happened to us when He rose?

Peter says it plainly: *"God . . . has caused us to be born again to a living hope through the resurrection of Jesus Christ from the dead"* (1 Peter 1:3, ESV). The heart of the gospel is this: when Jesus died, we died. And when He rose, we rose—with Him, to new life, there and then, 2,000 years ago.

Listen to how Paul describes it in Ephesians 2:

> But God, being rich in mercy, because of His great love with which He loved us, even when we were dead in our transgressions, made us alive together with Christ (by grace you have been saved), and raised us up with Him, and seated us with Him in the heavenly places in Christ Jesus. —Ephesians 2:4-6 (NASB)

The gospel is the astonishing news that something happened to the Son of God—and, in Him, something happened to the human race. If all fell in Adam, what happened when Jesus, the incarnate Son, died? Paul tells us: *we died with Him*. But that's just the beginning. When He rose, we rose. When He ascended to the Father's right hand—the place of love, delight, and full acceptance—we were lifted and seated with Him.

The gospel is the good news of what became of Jesus and what became of us in Him. In His death, burial, resurrection, and ascension, Adam and all of us were carried through death into new life and union with God.

The Cross was not an isolated act of sacrifice but part of a seamless movement in which the Triune God laid hold of humanity, cleansed our alienation, breathed new life into us, and lifted us into fellowship with Father, Son, and Spirit.

It is finished.[41]

---

41 Full chapter adapted from Baxter C. Kruger, *Jesus and the Undoing of Adam* (Jackson, MS: Perichoresis Press, 2007).

CHAPTER 11

Perfectly Upside Down

A Radical New Lens on Perfection

By Dr. Cory Rice

*P*erfection.
It's a word that carries weight. For many, it feels impossible—an unattainable standard that leaves us feeling like we'll never measure up. We live in a world obsessed with performance, where perfection is often defined as flawlessness, moral superiority, or the absence of mistakes. But what if we've misunderstood what perfection really means?
» What if being perfect isn't something we achieve but something we receive?
» What if it's not about striving, but about resting in a greater reality?

» What if perfection isn't about spotless integrity but about something deeper, something more liberating, something we're called to express?

This chapter is an invitation to rethink perfection—not as an impossible demand but as a divine gift. It's about stepping into the reality of who you already are in God's eyes. It's about understanding that perfection isn't about moral flawlessness but about love, mercy, and identity. Let's discover the joy and freedom of embracing perfection that is already within us because of Christ.

Have you ever been to a party and a dance battle broke out? If it's the right crowd, they're amazing to watch. If it's a middle-class Caucasian wedding, they're atrocious.

> *But does the world hear Christians dancing? Or do they hear Christians judging, protesting, and living offended?*

Dance battles are one reason I love movies like *Stomp The Yard*.[42] Yes, I know this movie is nearly twenty years old. But it captures something I love—the joy of movement, rhythm, and celebration.

In the story of the Prodigal Son in Luke 15, the older brother HEARD dancing at the party thrown for his

---
42 Sylvian White, *Stomp the Yard* (January 12, 2007; Culver City, CA: Sony Pictures).

younger brother. Heard them dancing? First-century Jewish dance parties must have been wild. I like to imagine Usher, Lil Jon, Ludacris, and Snoop Dogg showing up as the entertainment. Whatever the case, they were celebrating so hard you could hear the dancing!

That's the kind of joy the world should associate with believers—undeniable, infectious, and impossible to ignore. But does the world hear Christians dancing? Or do they hear Christians judging, protesting, and living offended?

In my opinion, people who follow Jesus should be the most entertaining, fun, creative, innovative, attractive, loving, and grace-filled people on the planet.

- » If people looked at our lives, would they want the Jesus we worship?
- » Do people feel valued and empowered by our presence?
- » Do we create safe spaces for dialogue and doubt?
- » Are we provoking the world to jealousy—not with self-righteousness, but with our freedom, peace, and joy?

Dietrich Bonhoeffer is believed to have said, "Your life as a Christian should make non-believers question their disbelief in God."

Maybe it's time for a shift in perspective. Maybe we just need to go dancing.

PROSTITUTES

I find it incredible how God empowered prostitutes throughout Scripture. Rahab, Gomer, Tamar, the Moabite and Midianite women, Jephthah's mother, the symbolic figures of Oholah and Oholibah, the two mothers in 1 Kings 3, and the woman with the alabaster jar—just to name a few. The inclusion of these women proves something revolutionary: God's perfection isn't about spotless morality. He wove their stories into His redemptive plan, proving that grace doesn't fit inside religious boxes.

> *We've been taught that claiming perfection is arrogant, but in reality, denying it is false humility.*

And honestly, I love that.

Because nothing upsets a religious mindset quite like the radical inclusivity of God's love and mercy.

You know what else offends religious thinking? The idea that God gives us perfection as a gift. He doesn't demand we earn it, strive for it, or clean ourselves up first. The finished work of Jesus means your failures can't undo what He has already secured.

Colossians 2:14 says He canceled our debt.

Hebrews 10:17 declares He remembers our sins no more. Psalm 103:12 tells us our transgressions are removed as far as the east is from the west.

John 1:29, Jesus is called "the Lamb of God who takes away the sin of the world"—not just individual sins, but the entire condition of sin itself.

We've been taught that claiming perfection is arrogant, but in reality, denying it is false humility. Many walk around saying, "I'm still in progress," but the truth is, you're not working your way toward perfection. You're already perfect in Him. Your journey is simply about learning to live in that truth.

God's fullness already dwells in you. His power is already within you. And that power—given freely—comes with the responsibility to use it well. Scripture is full of people who misused their God-given authority—Moses, Elijah, even David. But God's power isn't meant to control or condemn—it's meant to lift people up, to love without limits, and to bring heaven to earth.

Your actions don't determine your perfection in God's Kingdom. But they do affect how much of that Kingdom flows through you.

Jesus redefined perfection.

In Matthew 5:48 (NIV), Jesus said, "Be perfect, therefore, as your heavenly Father is perfect."

If we define perfection the way religion does, this statement becomes crushing. But in context, Jesus had just finished teaching about loving our enemies, doing good to those who harm us, and showing kindness beyond what is expected. So, what kind of perfection is He talking about? This isn't to be interpreted as an impossible and overwhelming command, believing we must strive for sinless performance. In Greek, the verb here implies a state of being, not a task to accomplish. Jesus wasn't commanding effort; He was inviting identity. He was inviting us to mirror Him.

Luke's account of this teaching (Luke 6:36) clarifies it even further: "Be merciful, just as your Father is merciful" (NIV). Perfection isn't about flawless behavior—it's about radical mercy. We are made perfect—not by our own efforts, but by His righteousness (Hebrews 10:14).

If God's perfection is marked by mercy, then our lives should reflect the same. In Matthew 19:21 (NIV), Jesus told the rich young ruler, "If you want to be perfect, go, sell your possessions and give to the poor." Jesus demonstrated this in everything He did: welcoming the outcast, forgiving sinners, healing the broken, empowering the poor. Mercy isn't just an act; it's a way of being. It's seeing people the way God sees them, responding with grace instead of judgment, and choosing love over condemnation.

To be perfect is to be merciful.

THE PURE IN HEART

In Matthew 5:8 (NIV), Jesus declares, "Blessed are the pure in heart, for they will see God."

At first glance, we might assume that purity of heart refers to moral perfection or the absence of sin. But Jesus wasn't talking about sinlessness—He was talking about something much deeper.

To be pure in heart is to be free from pride, hypocrisy, and judgmentalism. It's about having a heart that is undivided, sincere, and untainted by self-righteousness. The promise attached to this beatitude is that the pure in heart will *see* God. But what does that mean?

Jesus reveals that seeing God isn't just about an afterlife experience; it's about perception *now*. Seeing God isn't about physical sight; it's about spiritual vision. It's about seeing through the eyes of God.

The opposite of seeing is blindness, and throughout His ministry, Jesus repeatedly called the Pharisees *blind* because of their spiritual arrogance. Their pride, hypocrisy, and judgmentalism prevented them from recognizing God—even when He stood before them in the flesh.

In Matthew 5:8, Jesus was referencing Psalm 24:3-4 (NIV), which asked, "Who may ascend the mountain of the LORD? Who may stand in His holy place? The one who has clean hands and a pure heart." In Hebrew, the word for *heart* is lev, which refers to the *seed of the mind*—our thoughts, desires, and intentions. A pure heart, then, is not about moral purity, but rather seeing as God sees.

To be pure in heart is to be free from the distortions that cloud our vision—our biases, our tendency to judge, our assumptions about who is worthy and who is not. When our hearts are pure, our *sight* is clear. Instead of seeing people through the lens of their failures or shortcomings, we see them through the lens of God's love and mercy.

> ## We don't build the Kingdom— we participate in it.

This is why I believe the pure in heart are those who live out Acts 10:28 (NIV), where Peter, after a revelation from God, declares, "God has shown me that I should not call anyone impure or unclean."

When we stop labeling people based on external appearances or past mistakes, we begin to see them the way Jesus does.

Jesus ties together *heart* and *sight* in a profound way. The condition of our hearts determines the clarity of our vision.

- » A judgmental heart will always see flaws.
- » A self-righteous heart will always see sinners.
- » A pure heart—one free from pride and hypocrisy— will see God. Not in the heavens, but in the people around us, in the most unexpected places, and in the moments where grace and mercy are at work.

So how does perfection manifest?

It's in understanding the Kingdom of God is within. We don't build the Kingdom—we participate in it. The Kingdom is not an earthly kingdom but a spiritual kingdom that influences earth. Jesus told us a lot of what the Kingdom of God is like. Paul tells us what the Kingdom of God is in Romans 14:17—it's righteousness, peace, and joy. These are gifts, and when we embrace them, we walk in identity, inheritance, and influence:

- **Identity:** Knowing who you are. Righteousness is not something you get when you stop sinning. It's a gift. Righteousness is aligning who I am with who God says I am. You are a son or daughter of the King of Kings!
- **Inheritance:** Knowing what you have. There is a difference between receiving an inheritance by promise versus receiving an inheritance by performance. The most dangerous thing that can happen to you is that you become proud of your obedience. Like the father told the oldest son in the parable of the prodigal (Luke 15): "Everything I have is yours." You are already walking in the inheritance.
- **Influence:** Knowing how to equip and empower others. Our job is to remind people of who they have always been—God's beloved. You speak to the Son in people, not the sin in people. People don't have a sin problem. They have a belief problem because they refuse to see themselves the way the Father does. When we know our permanent position in the Kingdom of God because of what Jesus has done, it

empowers us to walk in the greatness God created us with. Your behavior will never dictate your position in the already present Kingdom of God. Jesus dictates your position, and He has already declared you royalty whether you believe it or not. Your behavior will, however, determine how much of the Kingdom of God flows through you. When you know who you are and the inheritance you already have, righteousness, peace, and joy will flow through you to everyone you meet.

THIS IS WHAT GREATNESS LOOKS LIKE

In a world obsessed with flawless appearances, Jesus invites us into a different kind of perfection—the perfection of mercy and love towards others. But are you merciful and loving towards yourself? When you know how great you are because a great God lives in you, mercy and love flow freely.

I wrote this in Day 21 of my devotional *What If I Told You?*:

> *"When you can't see the greatness you were born with, you will settle for less than your worth. You don't give God any honor by putting yourself down."*[43]

In Mark 10:35-45, we read James and John arguing over who is the greatest. We often miss an incredible revelation of true greatness once Jesus gets involved

---
[43] Cory Rice, *What If I Told You: A 21-Day Guide to Knowing Who You Are and Why It Matters* (The Writer's Society, 2023).

in the conversation. Jesus did not have a problem with their desire for greatness. He had a problem with what they thought greatness was. What's crazy is the same argument over who is the greatest happens again in Luke 22 during the last supper. Again, Jesus did not rebuke His disciples for wanting to be great. Instead, He showed them how—by washing their feet. True greatness empowers, serves, and loves others. Greatness is not about winning, controlling, or proving; it's about liberating, healing, and restoring. He showed them their perspective about greatness was jacked. Greatness in the Kingdom of God is not about climbing the ladder of success to gain a bigger title. It's about recognizing your title as a child of God and grabbing a bigger towel while creating a bigger table. When we wash feet, it's about lifting others up without putting ourselves down. It's about empowering people, not overpowering people.

Greatness is not about following Jesus to get into Heaven. It's about bringing Heaven to Earth!

For the record, Jesus knew Judas was going to betray Him, and He still washed his feet. The test of following Jesus is not how you love Jesus—it's how you love others, especially how you love Judas.

We must understand our greatness because a great God lives in us. Greatness requires discipline, and we must kill the idea that greatness looks different than being faithful to everyday life.

- » Greatness is simply serving and loving others from the overflow of being served and loved by God.
- » Greatness is in you, but it's expressed by serving and loving your spouse, kids, parents, friends, etc.
- » Greatness is recognizing that "normal" is okay.
- » Greatness is being a present spouse and parent.
- » Greatness is looking out for your friends and rejoicing at their success while also being a shoulder to lean on in their failures.
- » Greatness is about doing the millions of small things that bring accomplishment into the picture.
- » Greatness starts when you stop striving for a position you already have.
- » Greatness is recognizing how much God believes in you.

Greatness is not about following Jesus to get into Heaven. It's about bringing Heaven to Earth! It's about recognizing you have the power to bring Heaven into every room you walk into.

FOUR WAYS TO LIVE IN THE FLOW

When you recognize how great you are because a great God lives in you, mercy and love will flow naturally in four specific ways.

You are never more like God than when you are:

1) **Creating: Reflecting God's Creativity**

God is the ultimate Creator, and you are made in His image. That means creativity isn't optional; it's part of your design. But too often, fear and criticism silence our creative voice.

Don't let the doubts of others—or your own—keep you from bringing something new into the world. People who create give people who don't something to talk about. And even if what you create isn't "big" by the world's standards, it matters.

Maybe it's art, writing, or music. Maybe it's creating opportunities for people to connect. Maybe it's building new habits for a healthier, more fulfilled life. What is inside you that needs to be expressed? The world needs what you carry.

2) **Giving: Living with Open Hands**

Giving is about more than money—it's about offering your time, talents, and energy to lift others up. True giving isn't always convenient or aligned with our personal passions, but it is always powerful.

Sometimes, giving looks like generosity with your finances. Other times, it looks like lending your skills to help someone in need. It might mean being present for a friend who's struggling or taking the time to encourage someone.

Whatever it looks like, giving shifts your focus from self-preservation to abundance. The more you pour out, the more flows back in.

3) Restoring—Bringing Heaven to Earth

Restoration is the heart of God. It's what mercy looks like in action. To restore means to bring value where it has been lost, to lift up what has been torn down, and to see worth where the world sees none.

Jesus didn't just preach mercy—He *did* mercy. He healed the sick, fed the hungry, and embraced those society cast aside. Restoration isn't just a feeling; it's something we *do*.

Who in your life needs encouragement? Who has been overlooked? Where can you be a voice of hope? Living in the flow of God's mercy means stepping into the places that need healing and choosing to restore instead of judge.

4) Sustaining—Stewarding What You've Been Given

Sustaining isn't flashy. It's not always exciting or sexy. But it's essential.

You have dominion, power, and responsibility over what God has entrusted to you—your relationships, your calling, your health, your faith. While creating is about starting something new, sustaining is about maintaining what already exists. And maintenance requires work.

Too often, we overlook the power of consistency because it feels mundane. But sustaining is what turns moments into movements, ideas into realities, and dreams into lasting impact.

Sometimes, sustaining looks like showing up when you don't feel like it. Sometimes, it looks like tending to the small things no one else notices. But faithfulness in the unseen always leads to impact in the long run.

Perfection isn't about reaching a standard—it's about stepping into the flow of who you already are in Christ. It's about expressing the mercy of God to the world. When you create, give, restore, and sustain, you reflect the very nature of God.

Now, the only question is: How will you live in the flow?

CHAPTER 12

The Case for Universal Restoration

Constructing a Biblical Theology of Hell

By Keith Giles

Note: All bolded portions within Scripture quotes in this chapter represent emphasis added by the author to underscore key points and support the overall argument.

The doctrine of Universal Reconciliation, or Apokatastasis, is entirely biblical. In other words, the belief itself is rooted completely in the teachings of the Old Testament prophets, the apostles of the New Testament scriptures, and, of course, Jesus Himself.

This may come as a shock to many who have never studied the doctrine very closely, especially for those who have simply accepted the rhetoric often repeated from the pulpit that "No one ever spoke about hell more than Jesus did" or that "the Scriptures clearly teach that those who reject Christ will spend an eternity in hell," etc.

Not only are these sorts of claims false and misleading, they are inconsistent with what we see reflected in the Scriptures regarding God's reaction to sin, God's character and nature as revealed by Christ, and the explicit teachings from both Jesus and the Apostle Paul concerning the purpose of God's discipline and the goal of God's ultimate plans for those created in God's own image.

This short chapter will endeavor to illuminate some of the more prominent scriptures concerning these points, but unfortunately, we won't have the space here to cover all the verses that support the doctrine of Universal Reconciliation. So far, I have found over seventy-six verses in the Scriptures that support the notion of ultimate redemption for all humanity. Therefore, we will do our best to highlight the most relevant texts in the space we have available to us in this volume.[44]

From a purely Biblical perspective, what we see in the Hebrew Scriptures, commonly referred to as the Old Testament, is absolute silence on the subject of Eternal

---

[44] Note: My book, *Jesus Undefeated: Condemning the False Doctrine of Eternal Torment* (Quoir, 2019), covers most of the texts supporting Universal Reconciliation.

Torment. Simply put, the Jewish texts say nothing whatsoever about anyone suffering an eternity in the flames of Hell as punishment for their sins or for rejecting the testimony of God.

What we do find, however, are verses that expound upon the lovingkindness of God that "endures forever" (Psalm 136:1), and the favor of God that "is everlasting" (Psalm 30:5), and promises that God's desire is to prepare "for all people a feast" and to "swallow up death forever" (Isaiah 25:6-8), and that "all the nations of the earth shall be blessed" (Genesis 18:18; 12:3; 28:14), and that "every knee shall bow," and that "all mankind shall come and swear an oath of allegiance to God" (Isaiah 45:21-25), etc.

What's more, we find specific verses that declare God's promise not to take away a life [and to] devise plans so that the one banished from Him does not remain banished (2 Samuel 14:14).

We also find dozens of verses in those Old Testament scriptures which affirm, over and over again, that, in the end, "all the earth shall worship [God] And sing praises" (Psalm 66:4, NKJV, author addition), and that "The Lord will not cast off forever.... yet He will show compassion According to the multitude of His mercies" (Lamentations 3:31-32, NKJV).

Of course, the greatest scriptural source for the doctrine of Universal Reconciliation comes from the New Testament scriptures, and so that is where we will focus our attention now.

When some Christians read the red letters of the gospels where Jesus speaks of "coming judgment" and the place "where their worm does not die and the fire is not quenched" (Mark 9:48, ESV), or of the unrighteous as being sent away "into outer darkness" (Matthew 22:13, NKJV) or to be cast "into the everlasting fire prepared for the devil and his angels" (Matthew 25:41, NKJV), they wrongly assume that Jesus is speaking of where anyone goes after they die, and they miss the fact that, in every case, he is quoting Old Testament prophets who were using a common Jewish teaching style known as "apocalyptic hyperbole."

As we've already shown, those Old Testament prophets never spoke once about anything resembling the doctrine of eternal conscious torment. So, when Jesus uses language that echoes the words of Isaiah, or Jeremiah, or the other prophets, he is not speaking of what happens to anyone after they die. He is quoting those prophets and using that language to say exactly what they were saying: that a very real destruction was inevitable unless the people changed their behavior and listened to the warnings of the prophet.

So, when Isaiah warned Egypt (in Isaiah 19:1, ESV, author addition) that they would see the Lord God "riding on a swift cloud" and "[coming] to Egypt," it wasn't a literal statement. God did not actually mount a cloud pony and ride in the sky above Egypt. But invading armies *did* come against them, defeated them, and took many of them as captives.

When Jesus quotes Isaiah 66:24 (in Mark 9:43-48) and warns the people of His day about avoiding the fate where "their worm does not die and the fire is not quenched," they knew what He meant. They understood that by quoting the passage in Isaiah, Jesus was speaking of the exact same sort of judgment that would take place, not in some spiritual reality after they were dead, but in their own lifetime.

In fact, that passage where Jesus quotes Isaiah is actually speaking of those who would "go out and look on the dead bodies of the men who have rebelled against [God]" (ESV). So, those who rebelled are dead. They are not suffering torment. The fires are not quenched because—using hyperbole—the number of bodies is nearly endless, and the worm does not die because— once again—the source of food they consume in terms of dead bodies is practically without end.

What's more, the place where those dead bodies are thrown is literally, in the Greek, *Gehenna*, which is not an eternal spiritual place of suffering but a very real, literal valley [Hinnom] just outside the walls of Jerusalem.

If you want to know what God is really like, look at Jesus.

---

198 THE *Sacred* UNDOING

Once you understand Jesus's use of apocalyptic hyperbole in the gospels, these supposed references to eternal punishment can be more easily understood as references to real-world suffering at the hands of invading armies in response to the people's lack of repentance.

The fulfillment of those warnings came, just as Jesus predicted, within the lifetime of His listeners—roughly forty years later—when the Roman armies surrounded Jerusalem in 70 AD and destroyed the Jewish Temple, brought an end to the daily sacrifices, and brought about the "end of the age" (not the end of the world).[45]

So, if Jesus never actively taught the doctrine of endless torment, does that necessarily mean that He taught the doctrine of Universal Reconciliation?

Let's see if we can find evidence of ultimate reconciliation in the teachings of Christ.

When we examine the teachings of Jesus, what we find is quite startling, especially in terms of how He approaches the notions of forgiveness, judgment, and mercy.

When Jesus suggests that "if you've seen me, you've seen the Father" (John 14:9, author paraphrase), the implication is clear: If you want to know what God is really like, look at Jesus. So, when we look at Jesus, what we see is a God who forgives everyone, all the time, instantly, without waiting for anyone to confess or repent or even ask for forgiveness. Jesus always declares

---

[45] A more extensive exploration of apocalyptic hyperbole can be found in my books, *Jesus Unexpected*.

"your sins are forgiven" to everyone who comes to Him seeking to be healed or restored.

As New Testament scholar and author, David Bentley Hart observes:

If it is from Christ that we are to learn how God relates himself to sin, suffering, evil, and death, it would seem that he provides us little evidence of anything other than a regal, relentless, and miraculous enmity; sin he forgives, suffering he heals, evil he casts out, and death he conquers. And absolutely nowhere does Christ act as if any of these things are part of the eternal work or purposes of God.[46]

Jesus also declares in the Gospel of John 12:32 (author paraphrase and addition), that His mission is to literally drag (*helkuo* in the Greek), "all mankind to [Himself]."

We also find two quite shocking statements from Jesus where He says: "Moreover, the Father judges no one, but has entrusted all judgment to the Son" (John 5:2, NIV).

And then, surprisingly, He adds this startling admission a few chapters later: "I pass judgment on no one" (John 8:15, NIV).

So, if the Father judges no one but leaves that to the Son, and if the Son says, "I judge no one," where does that leave us? What are we to do with passages where Jesus famously speaks about the separation of the sheep and the goats in Matthew 25:41-46?

---

46 David Bentley Hart, *The Doors of the Sea: Where Was God in the Tsunami?* (Grand Rapids, MI: Eerdmans, 2011), 86-87.

> Then he will say to those on his left, "**Depart from me, you cursed, into the eternal fire prepared for the devil and his angels.** For I was hungry and you gave me no food, I was thirsty and you gave me no drink, I was a stranger and you did not welcome me, naked and you did not clothe me, sick and in prison and you did not visit me." Then they also will answer, saying, "Lord, when did we see you hungry or thirsty or a stranger or naked or sick or in prison, and did not minister to you?" Then he will answer them, saying, "Truly, I say to you, as you did not do it to one of the least of these, you did not do it to me." **And these will go away into eternal punishment, but the righteous into eternal life.** —ESV

This passage is probably the most often quoted by those who argue for eternal torment since it appears that Jesus equates the eternal quality of those being punished with the eternal duration of those being rewarded. We can't say the punishment isn't eternal without suggesting that the eternal life experienced by the righteous isn't also without end. Or can we?

The word "eternal" used twice in this passage is the Greek word *aionious*, and while it may often be used to suggest an endless duration of time, it is also quite frequently used in the Scriptures to describe events that are not endless but merely "a very long time."

For example, in the Greek translation of the Old Testament scriptures, the Hebrew word *olam* is translated into the Greek word *aionious* in Isaiah 32:14-15, which says:

> *The fortress will be abandoned, the noisy city deserted; citadel and watchtower will become a wasteland forever* [aionios], *the delight of donkeys, a pasture for flocks,* **till the Spirit is poured on us from on high, and the desert becomes a fertile field, and the fertile field seems like a forest.** —ESV (author addition)

Notice that while the fortress is prophesied to become an "abandoned ... wasteland forever" (using the Greek word *aionios*), that will last "until the Spirit is poured out on us," which means it wouldn't remain that way "forever" but merely "a very long time."

There are numerous other examples of this term *aionios* being used in this same way—to describe an event as lasting "almost forever" but not literally so.

The same is true for the Hebrew word *olam* which is used over 300 times in the Old Testament scriptures to indicate something that endures for a very long time but not necessarily without end. In at least twenty cases, the word *olam* is used to refer to events in the past. Therefore, *olam* and *aionios* are quite often used to refer to events that last a very long time, but are not necessarily without end.

Even someone like Francis Chan, who holds to the doctrine of eternal torment, admits in his book on this subject, *Erasing Hell*, that his confidence in the word *aionios* as a reference to something that is literally endless was shaken once he realized how often the term was used to describe events that were not always endless, saying:

"The debate about hell's duration is much more complex than I first assumed. While I lean heavily on the side that says it is everlasting, I am not ready to claim that with complete certainty."[47]

However, even if the term *aionios* was intended to suggest an endless quality of the fire in the Matthew 25 passage, we need to understand the nature of the fire as a metaphor for purification and restoration throughout the Scriptures.

Many of us have become so conditioned to read verses that speak of people being "thrown into the lake of fire" or subjected to "the eternal fire" of judgment, that we assume this must indicate either a state of endless suffering and torture, or the place where sinners are consumed and annihilated by God.

But is that the way this metaphor of God's fire is used in the Hebrew Scriptures or the New Testament? Not at all.

What we see in the Old Testament is the idea that God is "a consuming fire" that burns away our impurities and refines us into the original image of God found within every single one of us.

For example, in Malachi 3:2 (NIV), when speaking of the great and terrible Day of the Lord, where God comes to render a final judgment on the earth, here is what we find: "But who can endure the day of his coming? Who

---

[47] Francis Chan, *Erasing Hell: What God Said About Eternity, and the Things We've Made Up* (David C. Cook, 2011), 86.

can stand when he appears? **For he will be like a refiner's fire or a launderer's soap."**

The fire metaphor is equated with the quality of soap, which does not destroy or torture but makes us pure and clean. This is especially comforting when we read Jesus uttering words like this: "For everyone will be salted with fire" (Mark 9:49, ESV).

> *What the fire burns up is not us but the works which have not been consistent with the character and nature of Christ within each of us.*

No one will escape those flames of refinement or purification, according to Jesus, which is also what the Apostle Paul suggests in 1 Corinthians 3:14-15 (NIV, author addition) when he says this:

> [Everyone's work] *will be revealed with fire, and* **the fire will test the quality of each person's work.** *If what has been built survives, the builder will receive a reward.* **If it is burned up, the builder will suffer loss but yet will be saved**—*even though only as one escaping through the flames.*

This teaching is quite clear: Everyone will pass through the flames, both the righteous and the unrighteous. But what the fire burns up is not us but the works which have not been consistent with the character and nature of Christ within each of us.

We also find clues about the purpose and intention behind God's discipline and punishment in the book of Hebrews, where we read the following in Chapter 12, verses 7-11 (ESV):

> *It is for discipline that you have to endure.* **God is treating you as sons. For what son is there whom his father does not discipline?** *If you are left without discipline,* **in which all have participated,** *then you are illegitimate children and not sons. Besides this, we have had earthly fathers who disciplined us and we respected them. Shall we not much more be subject to the Father of spirits and live? For they disciplined us for a short time as it seemed best to them,* **but [God] disciplines us for our good, that we may share his holiness.** *For the moment all discipline seems painful rather than pleasant, but later* **it yields the peaceful fruit of righteousness to those who have been trained by it.** —(author addition)

Let's take a moment to notice what is being said here. First, the author of Hebrews says that God disciplines those He loves, and that this discipline is an indication of our identity as the sons and daughters of God, adding that we "all undergo discipline," which affirms that all of us are, indeed, the children of God. Next, he says that the reason God disciplines us is not for the sake of discipline itself, nor for the purpose of inflicting pain, nor to destroy us, but that God "disciplines us for our good, that we may share in [God's] holiness" and that this discipline leads to "the peaceful fruit of righteousness" for every single one of us.

So, whenever we read about anyone being cast into the flames of hell or the lake of fire, we must always keep in mind that this fire is intended to heal, restore, purify, and redeem us, never to harm us, or torture us, or destroy us.

Simply put, God's intention, as we read in various scriptures, is to "make all things new" and to "restore all things unto Himself." Jesus is heralded as the "Savior of the world" who intercedes on behalf of everyone—even those who murdered Him—by praying, "Father, forgive them, for they know not what they do."

No one is more vocal and emphatic about God's plan to redeem and restore all of humanity than the Apostle Paul. In fact, his statements are some of the most unmistakably universalist in tone than almost any others we find in the New Testament. Here are just a few examples:

> *For this is good and acceptable in the sight of our God our Saviour;* **Who will have all men to be saved, and to come to the knowledge of the truth.** *For there is one God, and one mediator between God and men, the man*

> Christ Jesus; **Who gave himself a ransom for all**, to be testified in due time. —1 Timothy 2:3-6 (KJV)

> This is a faithful saying and worthy of all acceptance. For to this end we both labor and suffer reproach, because **we trust in the living God, who is the Savior of all men, especially of those who believe.** These things command and teach. —1 Timothy 4:9-11 (NKJV)

> **For as in Adam all die, even so in Christ all shall be made alive.** —1 Corinthians 15:22 (NKJV)

> Just as the result of one trespass was condemnation of all men, **so also the result of one act of righteousness was justification that brings life for all men.** —Romans 5:18 (author paraphrase)

> God was pleased to have all fullness dwell in Him, **and through Him to reconcile to Himself all things on earth or in heaven**, by making peace through His blood, shed on the cross. —Colossians 1:19-22 (author paraphrase)

> For God was in Christ, **not counting our sins against us but reconciling the World to Himself.** —2 Corinthians 5:19 (author paraphrase)

We might also want to take a little more time with other passages from Paul's epistles, which equally affirm the doctrine of Universal Reconciliation in ways that we might not notice at first. Those are found in Philippians 2:10-11 and in Romans 11.

Let's start with what Paul says in Philippians:

> At the name of Jesus every knee should bow, of those in heaven, and of those on earth, and of those under the earth, and that every tongue **should gladly confess** that Jesus Christ is Lord to the glory of God the Father.
> —Philippians 2:10:11 (adapted from David Bentley Hart's translation)[48]

Notice that I've emphasized the phrase "should gladly confess" in this passage because our English translations of this text have sadly left out the entirety of the Greek word *exomologeo,* which literally means "to acknowledge openly and joyfully" rather than merely to confess. So, the text suggests that a day is coming when everyone will—of their own free will—gladly and joyfully acknowledge that Jesus is Lord, which is especially significant when you realize that in his epistle to the Romans, this same Apostle Paul affirms in Chapter 10, verse 9 that "If you confess with your mouth that Jesus is Lord... you will be saved."

The other emphatic passage where Paul exuberantly affirms the statement that all shall be saved is found in that same epistle to the Romans. But most of us miss this fact because we've been conditioned to read this letter

---

[48] David Bentley Hart, *The New Testament: A Translation* (Yale University Press, 2017).

a certain way. Specifically, we are not told that the letter was written using the rhetorical device of *prosopopoeia* in which the author communicates to their audience by speaking as another person having a conversation with someone who holds an opposing viewpoint. In other words, Romans is written as an imaginary debate between the Apostle Paul and another voice who, for all intents and purposes, is Saul the Pharisee.

Once we understand how this argumentation device is being used throughout the epistle of Romans, we start to notice how one voice declares a certain point of view, which the next voice refutes and corrects. It's an ongoing dialogue between the teacher of the Law and the Apostle of Christ regarding an important question: "Will all Israel be saved?" (see Romans 10)

As the two men debate back and forth, offering their perspectives and arguing their positions, the entire conversation culminates in Paul the Apostle concluding triumphantly that, yes, all Israel will be saved because God's plan is to save all people—both Jews and Gentiles—by extending saving mercy to everyone. Or, as Paul phrases it at the very end of Chapter 11 in verse 32 (NKJV): "For God has committed them all to disobedience, that He might have mercy on all."

And how does Paul celebrate his victory over his opponent in this long debate? By doing a little dance in the end zone, which immediately follows this verse above:

> *Oh, the depth of the riches both of the wisdom and knowledge of God! How unsearchable are His judgments and His ways past finding out! For who has known the mind of the LORD? Or who has become His counselor? Or who has first given to Him And it shall be repaid to him? For of Him and through Him and to Him are all things, to whom be glory forever. Amen.* —Romans 11:33-36 (NKJV)

But Paul is by no means the only apostle to speak so strongly of God's ultimate plan to redeem all mankind to Himself. We find in the letter of 1 John such wondrous verses like: "[Jesus] is the propitiation for our sins, and not for ours only but also for the whole world" (1 John 2:2, NKJV, author addition).

And in the Gospel of John: "[Jesus] did not come to judge the world but to save the world" (John 12:47, NKJV, author addition).

And in the Book of Hebrews: "Jesus, who was made a little lower than the angels, for the suffering of death crowned with glory and honor, **that He, by the grace of God, might taste death for everyone**" (Hebrews 2:9, NKJV).

And in the Book of Acts: "[In Jesus Christ is the] **restoration of all things**, which God has spoken by the mouth of all His holy prophets since the world began" (Acts 3:21, NKJV, author addition).

As I mentioned earlier in this chapter, there are over seventy-six different verses in the Bible that loudly affirm the doctrine of Universal Reconciliation, and we cannot explore each of them in as much detail as we might prefer in the limited space we have here.

However, by taking the time to share these verses that affirm Universal Reconciliation, I hope to make it clear that those who embrace this teaching do so not out of sentimentality nor by twisting the Scriptures to make them say what we want, nor by refusing to take the Bible seriously.

On the contrary, those of us who believe and teach the doctrine of Universal Reconciliation do so precisely because of what we read in the Old Testament scriptures, and what we hear from the mouth of Jesus, and what we see in the writings of the Apostle Paul, and John, and the Book of Acts, and Hebrews, and yes, even the Book of Revelation, about God's express desire and intention to redeem, restore, and reconcile every single one of us to Himself, not matter how long it takes.

Because the gates of God's Kingdom are never shut, and to those outside the walls the Spirit cries out, "Come and drink, all who are thirsty, from the rivers of living water that flow from the throne of God!" (Revelation 21:22-27; 22:1-5, 17)

Yes, God is that good. God is that loving. God is even more merciful and gracious than any of us could ever imagine.[49]

---

[49] Full chapter adapted from Keith Giles, *Jesus Undefeated: Condemning the False Doctrine of Eternal Torment* (London, UK: Quoir, 2019).

CHAPTER 13

Questions, Questions, Questions

Because Jesus Asked More Than He Answered

By Jamie Englehart

*D*id Jesus come to answer all of our questions, or did He come to give us more? The truth is not as black and white as I was raised to believe, and the Bible is not nearly as "clear" about many things as many like to teach, for life is full of gray areas. Jesus was actually asked more questions than He answered, and He also asked more questions than He answered. If you take the time to research this, what you will find is that Jesus was asked around 183 or so questions in Scripture. He only answered between three to eight questions, but He then asked nearly 340 more. I was rebuked by the President of a Bible college several years ago for ministering to the students by asking them questions. He said, "You need to minister the Word and stop ministering questions." I did not answer him for a few days because I took it to heart and did not want to harm anyone or teach error, and that is when I found those statistics, evidence that Jesus ministered more with questions than He did with clear answers. So, I answered him with: "I will stick with THE WORD, whereby He ministered questions." He wasn't trying to indoctrinate people with what to think, but teach them how to think for themselves. Jesus quotes the greatest commandment under the law in Luke 10:27 (NIV, emphasis added): "He answered, 'Love the Lord your God with all your heart and with all your soul and with all your strength and with all your MIND' and 'Love your neighbor as yourself.'" I do not think this is an accident or a mistranslation. He adds "mind," a word that is not found in Moses's command in Deuteronomy 6:5 (NKJV): "You shall love the LORD your God with all your heart, with all your soul, and with all your strength." In John 1:1 and 14, the beloved apostle uses the Greek word *logos*—where we get the word "logic" and "reason" from—to refer to Jesus the Son. Why? Because God wants us to join and reason together—He is not afraid of our questions.

Asking the right questions is what leads us to better answers.

First-century rabbis taught not just by giving answers but encouraging questions, discussion, and dialogue. I have a friend who studied with a Jewish Rabbi, and he mentioned to me one day that if you were to tell a Rabbi that you received personal revelation from Scripture, the Rabbi would ask, "Do you not have any friends?" They interpret Scripture in community, as does the Eastern Church to this day. Perhaps that is why the apostle Peter said in 2 Peter 1:20 (NKJV): "No prophecy of Scripture is of any private interpretation." There is wisdom in a multitude of counselors, and surrounding ourselves with others who ask questions keeps us from eisegesis and reading something into the text that is not there. Jesus, at twelve years old, confounds the teachers of the law in Luke 2:46-47 (NASB): "Then, after three days they found Him in the temple, sitting in the midst of the teachers, both listening to them and asking them questions. And all who heard Him were amazed at His understanding and His answers." They were amazed at His questions and His answers, for asking the right questions is what leads us to better answers.

The apostle Paul calls the mystery that was hidden from the ages, "Christ in you the hope of glory," and the mystery of Christ who is "all in all," so maybe we should be less dogmatic about our answers and start questioning some of them. If what we believe cannot hold up under the scrutiny of questioning, then we should not hold onto that belief too tightly. Let's be authentic enough to be intellectually honest about things we struggle with in Scripture. This younger generation is being indoctrinated against the Bible in our universities as they pick it apart in philosophy and ethics classes, and we have to learn not to be so defensive when we don't have all the answers. I hope that we all have wrestled with Moses saying that God commanded genocide, infanticide, the stoning of children, the tithing of virgins, and many more things that seem to paint God as less kind and moral than we are. Perhaps we should focus on being more Christ-like rather than being biblical literalists—always right, always trying to prove others wrong.

We now live in the information age, but many of us who are leaders were raised in the industrial age. It used to take me over a month just to order and pick up a book at a Christian bookstore, but now, I can push a button and read any book I want within seconds. One of my mentors taught me not to say to my children or grandchildren, "When I was your age," because we were never their age—only their years. I can relate to what a male child goes through physically at six years old, but he is being raised in a whole different world than when I was six. So, I was never his age. I was raised in an era where parents often answered their children's questions with, "because I said so," and church leaders often answered with, "don't touch God's anointed," as if we were questioning whether someone was of God or not. The younger generations' questions seem to threaten many older leaders who should instead embrace the practice of asking questions—just as the Jewish Rabbis and Jesus taught—as the most biblical way to learn. So rather than be intimidated, simply respond with, "That is a great question;" then, either give an answer or humbly admit you don't know it. "Let's look into that together" will go a long way. They will respect you even more when you are honest in admitting you don't know.

I am fifty-eight years old and do not seem to fit in the generation I was raised in because I was always asking questions and pushing the boundaries. So much that I was taught did not make sense to me, and my questioning nature has given me such a desire to grow and continually learn. I was told when I was just a young boy growing up in the Pentecostal Church that I had a questioning demon—a demon they never cast out of me or delivered me from—not that I wanted to be. I always thought that I would have more answers with age, but instead, I have found that I have more questions. As a young leader, I detested mystery because "I have the Holy Spirit who leads us into all truth," I would dogmatically declare, "so there shouldn't be any mystery" …right? Then I got older, and now, after thirty-six years of full-time traveling ministry and twenty-one years of leading a network of churches and ministries that has taken me to forty-seven states and twenty-six nations, I realize that there is so much I do not know, and the more I learn, the more I realize that I do not know. Maybe this is why, as an older man, Paul writes to the Philippians: "Brethren, I do not count myself to have apprehended; but one thing *I do*, forgetting those things which are behind and reaching forward to those things which are ahead, I press toward the goal for the prize of the upward call of God in Christ Jesus" (3:13-14, NKJV).

> **Peace in the midst of the mystery is more important than figuring everything out.**

We have all experienced grief and sorrow and have lost loved ones and friends and perhaps, at times, shouted at God, "WHY? If you are all-powerful and all-knowing, then why didn't you stop this from happening?" Perhaps the life of Jesus is less about answers and more about God descending as a human in the incarnation and walking with us in the mystery when we do not understand. Paul tells us in Philippians 4:7 (NKJV): "And the peace of God, which surpasses all understanding, will guard your hearts and minds through Christ Jesus." Peace in the midst of the mystery is more important than figuring everything out. Jesus, our Prince of Peace, guards our hearts and minds amid all the questions, fears, doubts, and misunderstandings, so make up your mind to move forward even in the midst of all of the questions. It's as if we are afraid to let people wrestle with God, Scripture, and their own unbelief rather than provide safe places to do that in our church cultures and organizations without fear and judgment. I want to encourage all leaders to at least open your hearts and minds to the possibility that none of us has God all figured out, and it is actually extremely arrogant to think we do. So, let's humble ourselves, embrace mystery, and continue to learn, unlearn, and relearn, for such is the Kingdom.[50]

---

50 Full chapter adapted from Jamie Englehart, "Faith in the Gray: Learning to Lead without Having All the Answers," AVAIL Journal, no. 23 (Fall 2025).

Permission to Wander

The Parable of the 99 Lost Sheep

By Martijn van Tilborgh

The first time we "meet" Jacob (in Genesis 25 and the chapters following), we learn about the cultural context that Jacob grew up in. The family dynamics and religious expectations were complicated (to say the least).

As a result, Jacob was conditioned to think that the only way to get access to "his father's blessing" was to pretend to be someone he was not.

In the short term, this approach appeared to work well. He received the blessing he so desperately desired, but only through a web of lies.

He wanted it so badly that he told himself that the hurt he caused other people in the process was just "the cost of doing business."

In other words, the end justified the means!

> *Away from "the flock," Jacob found the very thing he desired most in a way he couldn't have imagined.*

However, it didn't take long before his lack of authenticity caught up with him. His shenanigans were digging a hole for himself that would soon be too deep to climb out of.

Something had to change, or this was going to get him killed!

The only possibility to escape "certain death" was to leave his "safe place" that he had been familiar with his entire life.

It was scary, but removing himself from what had become a toxic environment was his only hope.

Instead of receiving the approval and affirmation he thought he needed, Jacob now found himself outside of the community he was once part of.

Like a "lost sheep," Jacob wandered off into the "wilderness."

And it was there, away from "the 99" (in a place where he least expected it), that he truly received "his father's blessing." Through a spiritual experience, in a place that he later called Bethel, he received something that exceeded his wildest expectations.

Away from "the flock," Jacob found the very thing he desired most in a way he couldn't have imagined.

Surprised by his experience, he cried out, "Surely the Lord is in this place, and I was not aware of it."

Wow, it was almost like Jacob got rewarded for his bad behavior!

All of this makes you wonder what it was about Jacob that "attracted" the blessing of God.

Perhaps it was more about Jacob's courage to leave his "cultural comfort zone" than it was about his "misconduct."

As I was pondering this, I asked myself a question.

Is it possible that Jacob is just a mirror that shows us a true reflection of ourselves?

Could it be that in some way we are all like Jacob in that we compare ourselves to others constantly while pretending to be like them to receive approval?

Are we also putting on "our brother's clothes" and "covering our arms with fur" to trick "our father" into blessing us?

I know I've been guilty of this, and I'm sure I'm not the only one!

Perhaps that's just part of everyone's journey. We all lack authenticity when we just start out in life. We all mimic others in a desperate attempt to gain "divine" (and human) approval.

We just can't stay there!

Maybe we need to consider the possibility that God encourages us to "wander off" from the rest of the sheep to discover who we truly are.

We should at least consider the possibility that sticking with the flock might simply perpetuate (or even strengthen) our inauthentic selves.

Because if that's true, it totally flips the script on the parable of the "lost sheep" (kinda like that green evil witch from the movie *Wicked*).[51]

Maybe that "lost sheep" wasn't as lost as we think he was.

Perhaps surprisingly, "the 99" were the ones that were lost. Or, at the very least, stuck in a place that encourages them to be something they are not.

Maybe not all who wander are lost!

There's something that I have observed about "religious culture." The more you are "in" with that specific religious culture, the more you start to look like everyone else that is "in." You start acting the same, talking the same, dressing the same.

I know you know what I'm talking about.

Did "the 99" stop being curious?

---

51 Jon M. Chu, *Wicked* (November 22, 2024; Universal City, CA: Universal Pictures).

Did they settle for second (or third) best?

Did they lack the courage (or desire) to explore a reality outside of their comfort zone?

Was the "lost sheep" just frustrated with "the same old life within the fold"?

Was he simply tired of "pretending"?

And was that maybe a good thing?

It definitely appears that the shepherd was more attracted to the "lost sheep" than he was to the rest of the flock. So much so that he leaves the 99 unprotected in the open country, determined to meet the "lost sheep" in his time of need.

Scripture even tells us that the shepherd was "HAPPIER about that one sheep than about the 99 that did not wander off" (literal quote from Matthew 18:13).

All of this leaves us with something to consider ... and that is that ...

Maybe not all who wander are lost!

And maybe that's the real invitation—not to settle in the comfort of the fold, but to have the courage to follow the questions, the restlessness, and the hunger that stirs in your soul. This book may have handed you a few tools, a handful of keys, or a fresh way of seeing, but they are only for the road ahead. You are not meant to stay here. You are free to step out beyond the fences of what you've known, to seek the ambiguous God in the wild places where certainty has no map. The same God who told Moses, *"I am who I am,"* still refuses to fit neatly into our definitions. He will be who He will be as you go, revealing Himself in ways you could not have anticipated.

So go ahead. Wander. Search. Pay attention to the moments that make you say, "Surely the Lord is in this place, and I was not aware of it." Trust that the Shepherd is not nervous about your journey—He delights in it. Like Moses, you will discover that the God who was and the God who is are only the starting points; there is also the God who is to come. This is the God who invites you into the unfolding story, a God who meets you both inside the fold and far outside it, where the path is not marked and the scenery constantly changes.

Because maybe—just maybe—the next step you take away from the flock is the one that will bring you face-to-face with Him. The ambiguous God will meet you there, not with the final answer, but with an open-ended invitation to keep discovering. And in that discovery, you may just find that wandering with Him was the point all along.

www.ingramcontent.com/pod-product-compliance
Lightning Source LLC
Chambersburg PA
CBHW050901160426
43194CB00011B/2245